Hsien tai chung-kuo hua chi tsui

現代中國畫集粹

T4-AXU-744

A SELECTION OF CONTEMPORARY CHINESE PAINTINGS

DISCARDED

UWEC McIntyre Library
SEP 9 1983
EAU CLAIRE, WI

朝 華 出 版 社 北京 1981年

ZHAOHUA PUBLISHING HOUSE Beijing 1981

Jacket: Sword Orchid by Chen Peiqiu
Painted on fan-covering in silk (1973 Diameter 32 cm)

Title: Inscribed by Xie Zhiliu

Edited and designed by Sun Jie

Chinese-English translation written by Hsu Menghsiung

First Edition 1981

Compiled and Published by ZHAOHUA PUBLISHING HOUSE
21 Chegongzhuang Xilu, Beijing

Printed by Zhong Hua Printing House
477 Aomen Road, Shanghai

Bound by Shanghai Bindery
554 Hongqiao Road, Shanghai

Distributed by GUOJI SHUDIAN (China Publications Centre)
21 Chegongzhuang Xilu, Beijing

Printed in the People's Republic of China

84 CE-552

OVERSIZE
ND
1045
.H845
c.1

前　　言

中國畫是具有悠久歷史和優良傳統的中國民族繪畫，在世界美術領域裏它自成獨特體系，深爲人們所喜愛。近些年來，隨着我國與世界各國文化交流不斷發展，各國來華訪問、旅遊人數不斷增加，人們對中國畫的興趣愈來愈濃。但由於過去對中國畫這門繪畫藝術介紹得不够，因而許多喜愛中國畫的朋友，對它還不很了解，希望我們能出版一本介紹中國畫藝術的出版物。

前些時，我們得知中國著名山水畫家宋文治三十多年來收藏了許多中國現代畫家的真跡。這些藏品筆墨蒼潤，構圖新穎，是欣賞和學習的精品。經徵得宋文治先生的同意，並在他的贊助下，從藏品中選了六十多幅編集成册，介紹給廣大的中國畫愛好者。

宋文治先生藏畫，當初是爲了學畫，收集來了可以借鑒學習。用宋文治先生的話來説："求得佳作，置於案頭，值時可讀，信手可翻，似師似友，獲益非淺"。爲此，他在與當代前輩和同道畫友交往時，化了很大精力，索求或交换到了許多精品，年長日久，成了一位畫家兼"藏家"。在客觀上他爲繪畫珍品的保存流衍出了力，還起到了嘉惠後人的作用。

我們編輯出版這本畫册，是爲了便於中國畫愛好者欣賞和學習中國畫的筆墨技法。因此所選的作品，大都是尺幅不大的軸畫、册頁畫和扇面，包括有用工筆、寫意、鈎勒、没骨、水墨等不同技法畫成的人物、山水、花卉、禽鳥、走獸、蟲魚等畫幅。還請中國著名美術理論家黄苗子先生撰文，論述中國畫的藝術特色，並對本畫册所收入的每幅畫和它的作者作簡要的介紹。

願這本畫册的出版能爲廣大中國畫愛好者提供有益的素材。

PREFACE

Chinese painting has a long history and an excellent tradition. In the field of fine arts it has a style of its own, delightful and pleasing. In recent years, as cultural exchange between China and foreign countries has developed and visitors and tourists from abroad are on the increase, universal interest in Chinese painting has steadily deepened. However, it is regrettable that too little work has been done to introduce Chinese painting to the Western world while those who have a liking for it have a strong desire to understand more about it. It is to meet this need that we have the pleasure of bringing out this album.

We have been fortunate enough to know that Mr. Song Wenzhi (宋文治), a famed artist and connoisseur of Chinese paintings, has for the last thirty-odd years collected a good many genuine works, all of which look vigorous, rich and full, and are composed in a novel and unique style. They are objects of learning as well as enjoyment. With his agreement and support we have selected sixty-eight paintings from his rich collection and present them here for lovers of Chinese fine arts.

Years ago Mr. Song started collecting contemporary masterpieces in order to learn the art of painting from them. He says, "I obtained good paintings, placed them on my desk, studied them at free moments, and leafed through them fondly. They were as good as my friends and teachers, and I profited from them a great deal." For the better part of his life he went among his friends and collectors in search of valuable paintings, buying and trading. Eventually he became a collector himself as well as a painter. We have good reason to say that Mr. Song has done very much to preserve and popularise rare paintings and to hand down to posterity a source of human delight in creative arts.

In compiling this album we have had in view the aim of satisfying the demand among lovers of Chinese painting for references that will enable them to enjoy and learn the skill of Chinese-ink painting. Our selection is limited to small-size scroll-painting, album-painting and fan-painting. This album contains paintings of figures, mountains and water, flowers, birds, four-footed animals, worms and fish. Various techniques are used, including fine brushwork with attention to detail, broad strokes for essence and spirit, and water-ink. Mr. Huang Miaozi (黄苗子), the well-known fine arts theorist, has contributed to this album a highly valuable article treating of the characteristics of Chinese art and giving a brief introduction to each painting and the painter.

It is our hope that this album will supply lovers of Chinese painting with source materials.

畫　　頁
Paintings

1. 齊白石　荷花鴨子　軸　紙本　1948年作
縱100厘米　橫34厘米

Qi Baishi: Lotus and Duck
Vertical scroll Mounted on paper 1948
Length 100 cm. Width 34 cm.

2. 齊白石　蔬菜草蟲　軸　紙本　1946年作
縱 30 厘米　橫36厘米

Qi Baishi: Chinese Cabbage and Turnip
Horizontal scroll Mounted on paper 1946 Length 30 cm. Width 36 cm.

3. 李可染　暮韻圖　軸　紙本　1977年作
縱 69 厘米　橫47厘米

Li Keran: Idyllic Evening *Vertical scroll Mounted on paper 1977 Length 69 cm. Width 47 cm.*

暮韻圖

4. 潘天壽　牡丹蝴蝶
長卷　紙本　1965年作
縱21.5厘米　橫95厘米

Pan Tianshou: Peony and Butterfly *Long scroll Mounted on paper 1965 Length 21.5 cm. Width 95 cm.*

5. 潘天壽　牡丹蝴蝶(局部)

Pan Tianshou: Peony and Butterfly *(detail)*

6．傅抱石　陶淵明詩意　册頁　紙本　1963年作
縱27厘米　橫35厘米

Fu Baoshi: Tao Yanming's Poem in Painting
Leaf from an album　Mounted on paper　1963
Length 27 cm. Width 35 cm.

7．葉淺予　和闐裝　軸　紙本　1977年作　縱46厘米
橫34厘米

Ye Qianyu: Xinjiang Costume *Vertical scroll*
Mounted on paper　1977　Length 46 cm.
Width 34 cm.

9．錢松喦　菊蟹圖　册頁　紙本
1959年作　縱·27 厘米　横35厘米

Qian Songyan: Chrysanthemums and Crab *Leaf from an album Mounted on paper 1959 Length 27 cm. Width 35 cm.*

10．錢松喦　菊蟹圖(局部)

Qian Songyan: Chrysanthemums and Crab *(detail)*

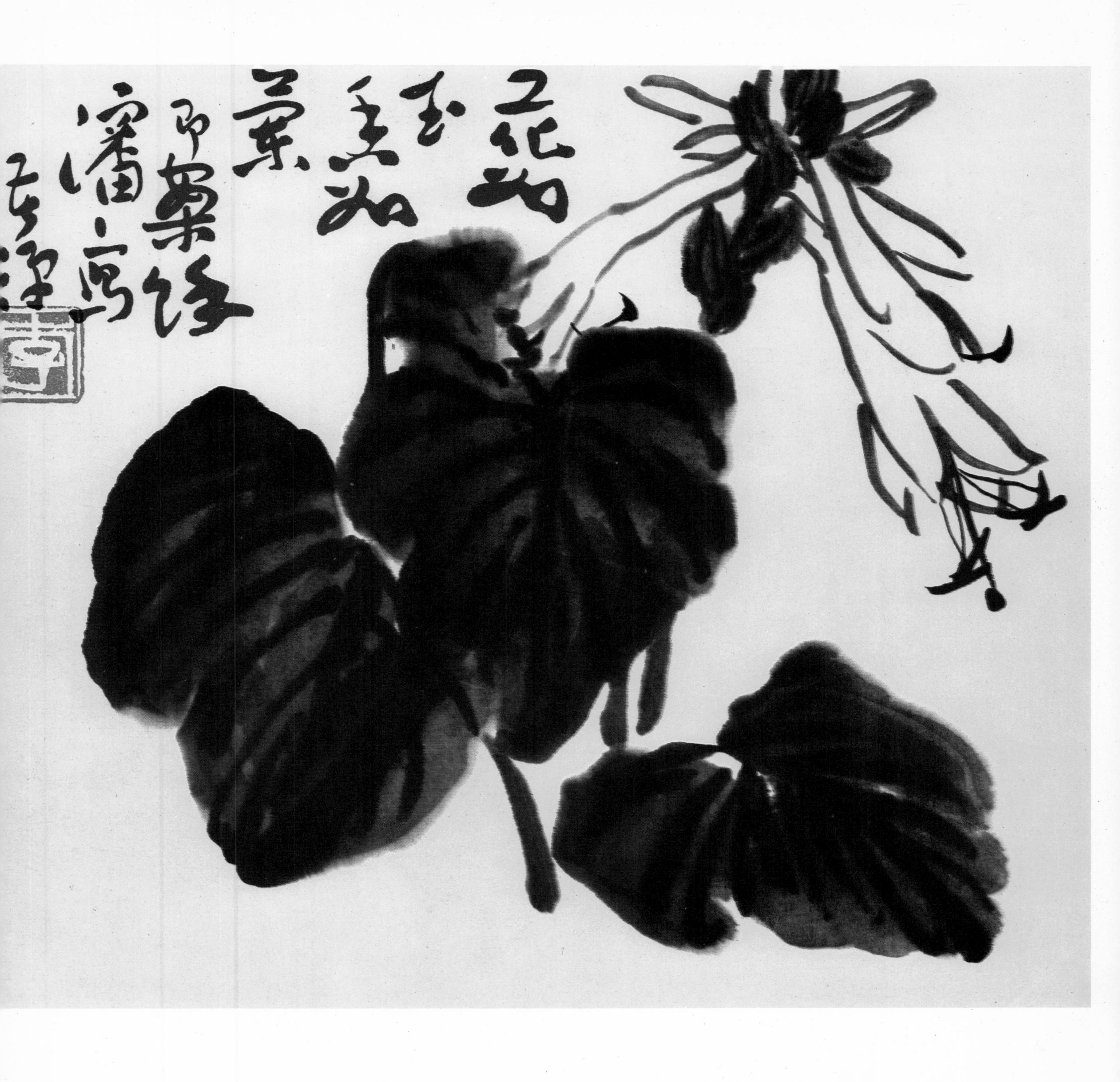

11. 李可染　淡墨山水　册頁　紙本　1977年作
縱32厘米　横25厘米

Li Keran: Landscape in Pale Inking *Leaf from an album Mounted on paper 1977 Length 32 cm. Width 25 cm.*

12. 李苦禪　玉簪花　册頁　紙本　1974年作
縱28厘米　横32厘米

Li Kuchan: Fragrant Plantain Lily *Leaf from an album Mounted on paper 1974 Length 28 cm. Width 32 cm.*

13. 李苦禪　松鷹圖　軸　紙本　1977年作　縱33厘米　橫60厘米

Li Kuchan: Pine and Hawk *Horizontal scroll Mounted on paper 1977 Length 33 cm. Width 60 cm.*

陸儼少

己未三冬
写故乡人物
卢沉

18. 亞 明　雪山圖　册頁　紙本　1978年作　縱34厘米　橫27厘米

Ya Ming: Snowy Mountain *Leaf from an album　Mounted on paper 1978　Length 34 cm.　Width 27 cm.*

20. 江
195

Jian
Autu
Moun
Lengt

23．陳佩秋　青蛙　册頁　紙本　1974年作　縱26厘米
横34厘米

Chen Peiqiu: Frog on Rock *Leaf from an album*
Mounted on paper 1974 Length 26 cm.
Width 34 cm.

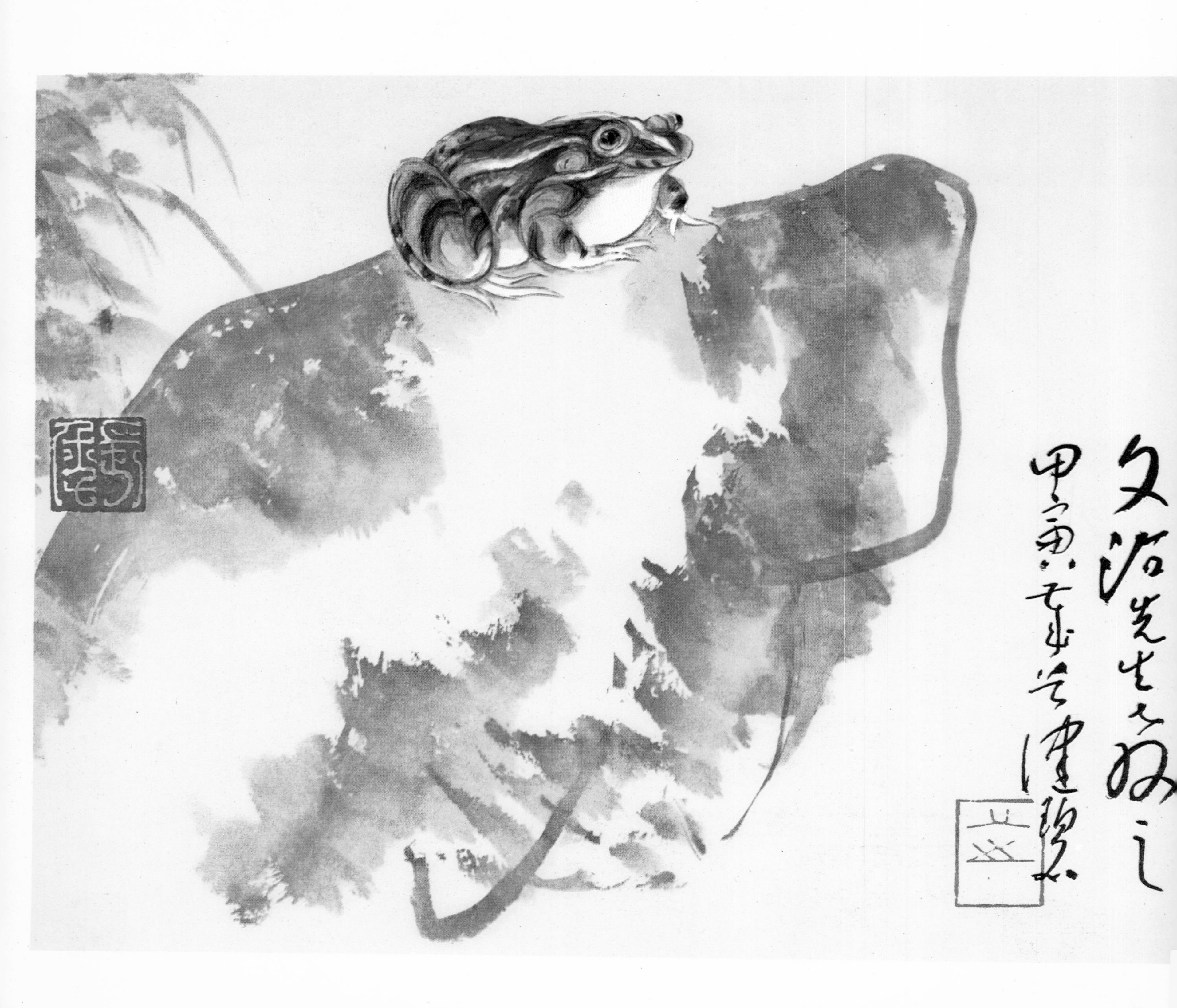

24．程十髮　鍾馗小妹圖　軸　紙本　1978年作
縱49厘米　橫47厘米

Cheng Shifa: Zhong Kui and His Sister *Vertical scroll　Mounted on paper　1978　Length 49 cm. Width 47 cm.*

25. 吴作人　犛牛圖　册頁　紙本　1977年作
縱28厘米　横35厘米

Wu Zhoren: Yaks *Leaf from an album　Mounted on paper　1977　Length 28 cm. Width 35 cm.*

26. 鄧　林　松枝黄花　軸　紙本　1978年作　縱68厘米
横46厘米

Deng Lin: Pine Needles and Day Lilies
Vertical scroll　Mounted on paper　1978
Length 68 cm. Width 46 cm.

27. 吴湖帆　墨 松　軸
紙本　1944 年作
縱 68 厘米　横35厘米

Wu Hufan: Pine
Vertical scroll Mounted on paper 1944 Length 68 cm. Width 35 cm.

28．關山月　紅梅　册頁　紙本　1974年作　縱28厘米　橫35厘米

Guang Shanyue: Red Plum Blossoms *Leaf from an album Mounted on paper 1974 Length 28 cm. Width 35 cm.*

29．陸儼少　川江險水圖　長卷　紙本　1975年作
縱32厘米　橫125厘米

Lu Yanshao: Treacherous Waters of a Sichuan River *Long scroll Mounted on paper 1975 Length 32 cm. Width 125 cm.*

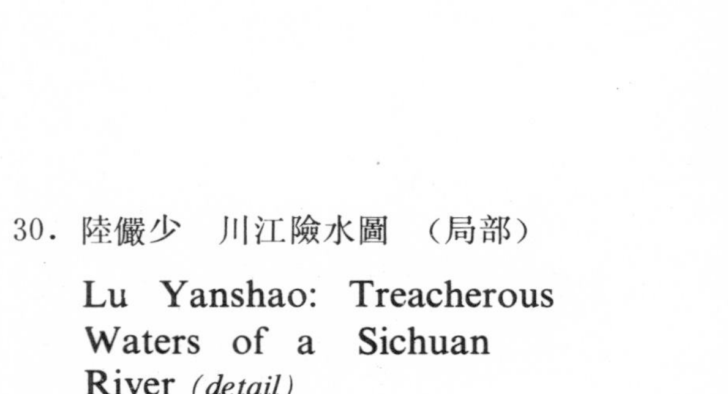

30．陸儼少　川江險水圖　（局部）

Lu Yanshao: Treacherous Waters of a Sichuan River *(detail)*

31. 鄭乃珖　春艷　軸　紙本　1973年作　縱54厘米
橫41厘米

Zheng Naiguang: Spring Beauty *Vertical scroll*
Mounted on paper　1973　Length 54 cm.
Width 41 cm.

32. 來楚生　松鼠山楂　册頁　紙本　1963年作
縱28厘米　橫35厘米

Lai Chusheng: Squirrel and Hawthorns
Leaf from an album　Mounted on paper　1963
Length 28 cm. Width 35 cm.

33．葉淺予　獻花舞　册頁　紙本　1977年作　縱32厘米　横25厘米

Ye Qianyu: Flower Dance *Leaf from an album Mounted on paper 1977 Length 32 cm. Width 25 cm.*

34. 魏紫熙　深山幽谷圖　册頁　紙本　1973年作
縱28厘米　橫35厘米

Wei Zixi: Mountain and Gully *Leaf from an album　Mounted on paper　1973　Length 28 cm. Width 35 cm.*

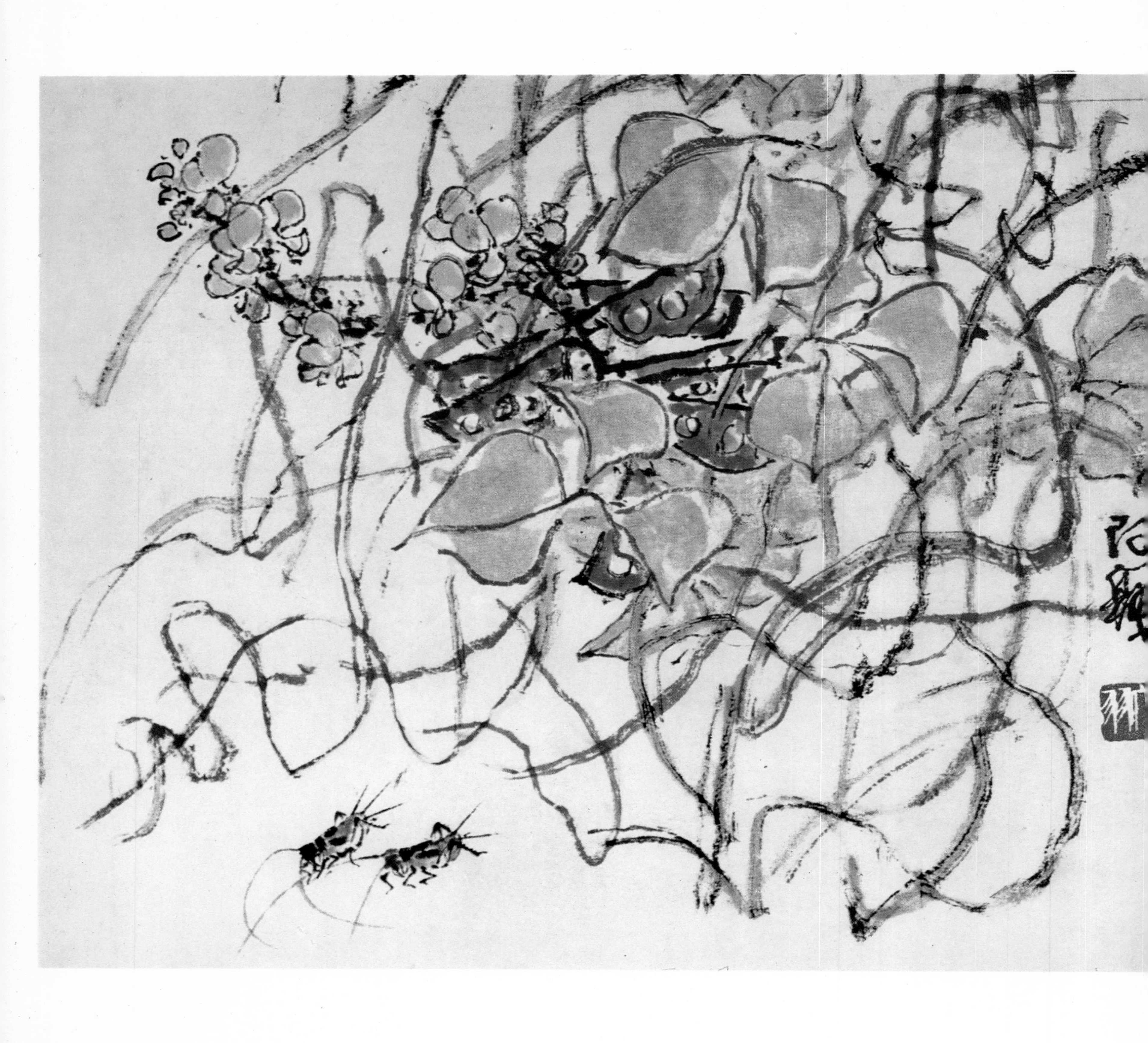

35．陳大羽　扁豆蟋蟀圖　册頁　紙本　1972年作
縱28厘米　横40厘米

Chen Dayu: Catalpa Pods and Crickets *Leaf from an album Mounted on paper 1972 Length 28 cm. Width 40 cm.*

36. 羅叔子　紅山茶　軸
紙本　1954年作
縱90厘米　橫46厘米

Luo Shuzi: Red Camellias *Vertical scroll Mounted on paper 1954 Length 90 cm. Width 46 cm.*

37. 黄 胄 駱駝 軸 紙本 1973年作 縱60厘米 橫64厘米

Huang Zhou: Camel *Horizontal scroll Mounted on paper 1973 Length 60 cm. Width 64 cm.*

一九七三年五月黃胄試用遷安紙作
黃胄

38. 王雪濤　令箭荷花　軸
紙本　1965年作　縱80厘米　橫40厘米

Wang Xuetao: Cactus Bloom *Vertical scroll*
Mounted on peper 1965
Length 80 cm. Width 40 cm.

41. 應野平　黄山清涼台　軸　紙本　1978年作　縱60厘米　横46厘米

Ying Yeping: Cool Mount Huangshan *Vertical scroll Mounted on paper 1978 Length 60 cm. Width 46 cm.*

42. 王个簃　石榴　册頁　紙本　1975年作　縱28厘米　橫35厘米

Wang Geyi: Pomegranates *Leaf from an album Mounted on paper 1975 Length 28 cm. Width 35 cm.*

43. 周思聰　新疆哈薩克族婦女　軸　紙本　1979年作　縱68厘米　橫46厘米

Zhou Sichong: Xinjiang Woman *Vertical scroll Mounted on paper 1979 Length 68 cm. Width 46 cm.*

文治先生正
己未思聰
周

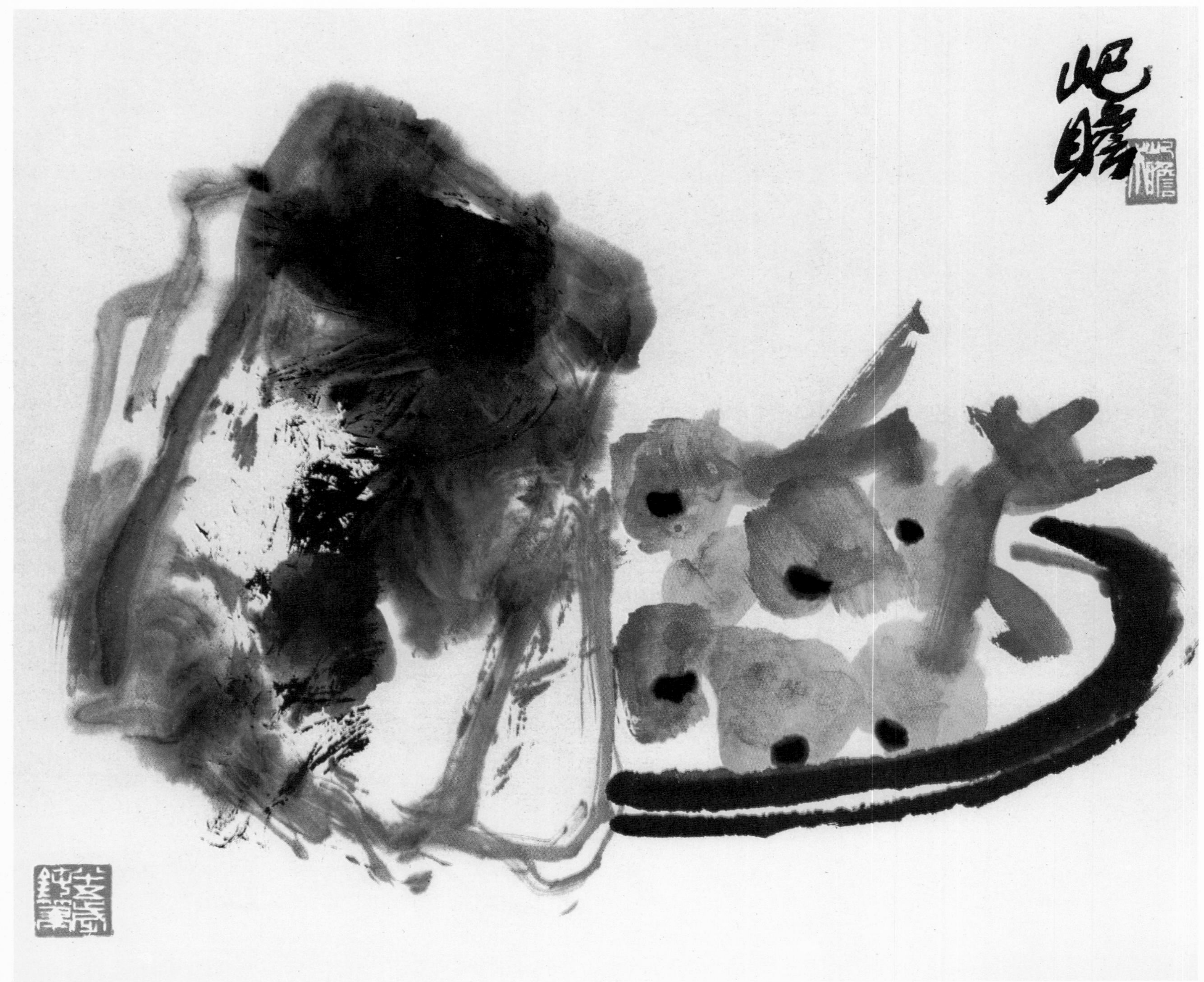

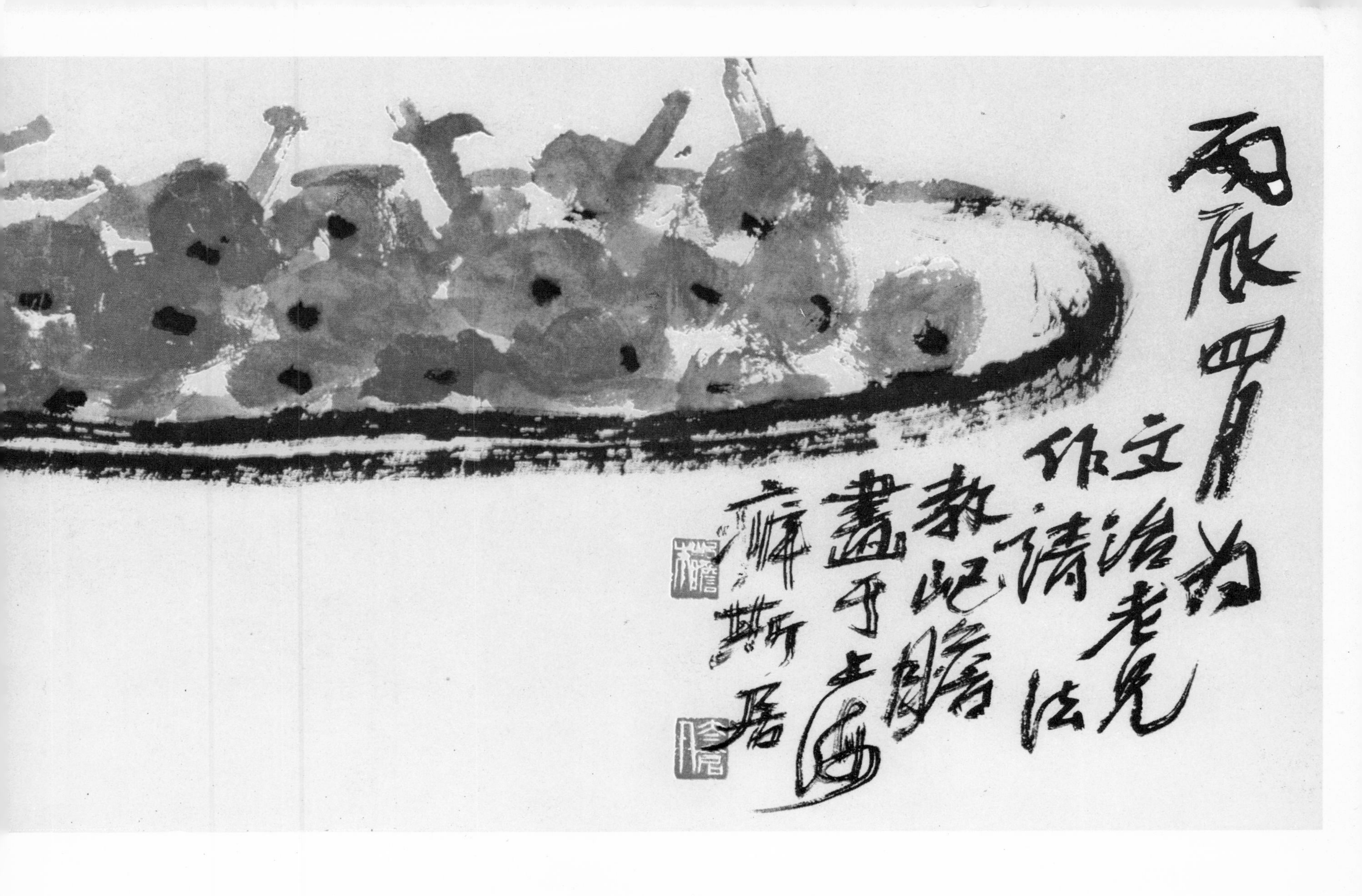

44. 朱屺瞻　枇杷粽子　長　卷　紙本　1976年作
縱 27厘米　橫92厘米

Zhu Qizhan: Loquats and *Zongzi* *Long scroll Mounted on paper 1976 Length 27 cm. Width 92 cm.*

45. 朱屺瞻　枇杷拳石　册頁　紙本　1976年作
縱28厘米　橫35厘米

Zhu Qizhan: Loquats and Rock *Leaf from an album Mounted on paper 1976 Length 28 cm. Width 35 cm.*

▼ 46．陳子奮　芙蓉花和蟹　册頁　紙本　1973年作
縱28厘米　橫39厘米

Chen Zifen: Cottonrose and Crab *Leaf from an album　Mounted on paper　1973　Length 28 cm. Width 39 cm.*

47．賀天健　玉簪花　册頁　紙本　1957年作　縱23厘米
橫36厘米

He Tianjian: Fragrant Plantain Lilies *Leaf from an album　Mounted on paper　1957　Length 23 cm. Width 36 cm.*

48．錢瘦鐵　墨梅　册頁　紙本　1962年作　縱30厘米
橫40厘米

Qian Shoutie: Plum Blossoms *Leaf from an album　Mounted on paper　1962　Length 30 cm. Width 40 cm.*

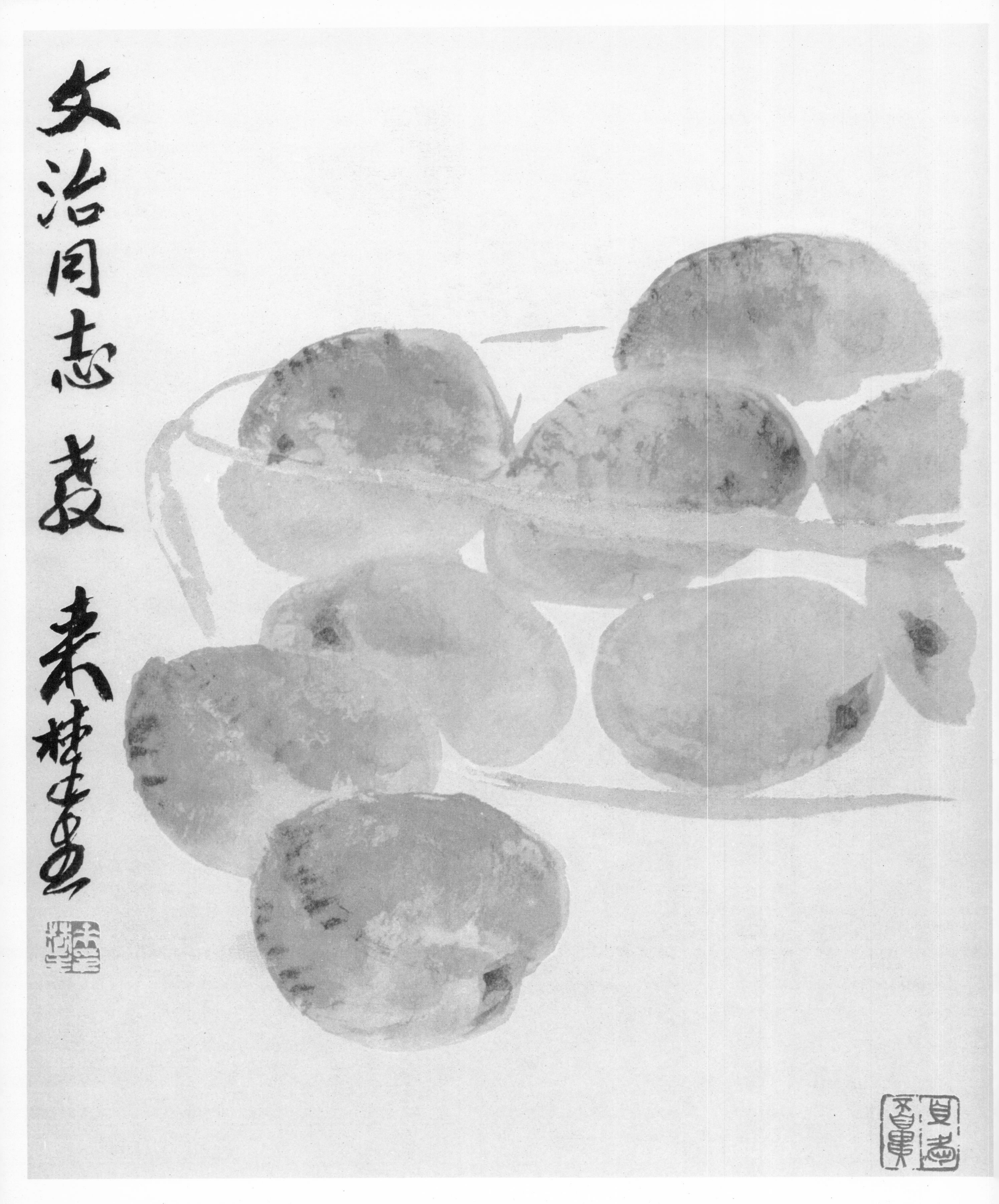

49．來楚生　水蜜桃　册頁　紙本　1963年作　縱32厘米
橫25厘米

Lai Chusheng: Honey Peaches *Leaf from an album Mounted on paper 1963 Length 32 cm. Width 25 cm.*

50. 林風眠　白鷺　軸　紙本　1965 年作　縱 42 厘米 横 48厘米

Lin Fengmian: Egret *Vertical scroll　Mounted on paper　1965　Length 42 cm. Width 48 cm.*

療饑畫于臨江日記 廣

▼ 57. 黄　胄　群驢圖　軸　紙本　1964年作　縱33厘米　橫48厘米

Huang Zhou: Donkeys *Horizontal scroll Mounted on paper 1964 Length 33 cm. Width 48 cm.*

58. 王雪濤　雄鷄牽牛花　軸　紙本　1964年作　縱47 厘米　橫60厘米

Wang Xuetao: Cock and Morning Glories *Horizontal scroll Mounted on paper 1964 Length 47 cm. Width 60 cm.*

59. 張正宇　猫　軸　紙本　1973年作　縱33厘米　橫34厘米

Zhang Zhengyu: Cat *Horizontal scroll Mounted on paper 1973 Length 33 cm. Width 34 cm.*

60．程十髮　茶花雙鳥　册頁　紙本　1978年作
縱27厘米　橫37厘米

Cheng Shifa: Camellias and Two Birds *Leaf from an album　Mounted on paper　1978　Length 27 cm. Width 37 cm.*

扇　　面
Fan-coverings

扇子是人們日常生活中常用的工具，也是中國傳統藝術品的一種形式。中國歷代文人在扇面上作詩繪畫，也已經有一千多年的歷史。宋、元流傳至今的扇面，大都是用細絹制成的圓形團扇或紈扇。明代以後，折扇已逐漸流行，直至今日，風氣衍盛，影響頗深。其中名家所作，已成爲中國重要的文化遺産。

折扇扇面的形狀是上寬下窄，呈半圓形。因此，作畫時必須在這種特定形狀内，匠心獨運地經營位置。一般是在折扇上寫字要依照折紋歸行書寫，作畫就不能這樣，而要保持一定的垂直和水平的方向；構圖也可不受折扇外形的約束，但又要和外形配合；用色則應考慮到扇面是近看的小品，和册頁同爲手中欣賞之物，因此作畫宜淡不宜深；所作的畫，要畫得精細、淡雅、輕松。此外，還要克服扇面在製作過程中，爲使表面平整光潔敷有一層膠矾，畫時就要有相應的表現技法，方能做到筆隨意轉，在咫尺之中，開拓妙趣盎然的意境。

這裏所選的十三幅扇面，都出自現代名家的精品。

Fans are useful items in summer. They are at the same time a form of traditional Chinese art. Men of letters and painters down the ages have written their poems and drawn their pictures on fans, and this artistic form has nearly a thousand-year history. Fans that date back to the Song and Yuan dynasties are round in shape and made of fine plain silk. From the Ming dynasty to the present, these have been in vogue, and their artistic qualities have had an impact on Chinese painting. Among them the products of distinguished calligraphers and painters have become an important part of the Chinese cultural heritage.

A folding fan is broad at the top and narrow at the bottom, making a semi-circle. Within this limited space of its covering the painter has to manoeuvre for background and foreground, setting and perspective, measurement and proportion of artistic creation. Generally speaking, a folding fan admits of calligraphy on its covering insofar as the brush-strokes can follow the folding creases. It is, however, not the case with a picture, which must keep varying degrees of verticality and levelness. Nor should the composition of a picture be restricted by the shape of the covering, as the two aspects must be in co-ordination. Colours and tints should be applied with the fact in mind that the picture will be on a fan which like an album, is to be viewed at very close range. It will be better, therefore, in light colours and an exquisite yet simple and easy style.

Moreover, as the fan covering is smoothed over with a film of gum, the painter must adapt his skill to this surface so that his pen can follow in creating the delightful scene or intriguing situation in his mind.

The thirteen coverings displayed in this album have been reproduced from famous contemporary painters' works.

61．齊白石　紫藤蜜蜂　紙本　1936 年作　縱 19 厘米　橫50厘米

Qi Baishi: Wistaria and Bees *Mounted on paper 1936 Length 19 cm. Width 50 cm.*

62. 黄賓虹　山水　紙本　1926年作　縱18厘米　橫50 厘米

Huang Binhong: Landscape　*Mounted on paper　1926　Length 18 cm. Width 50 cm.*

63. 傅抱石　行吟圖　紙本　1963年作　縱19厘米　橫50厘米

Fu Baoshi: Poet Reciting as He Strolls　*Mounted on paper　1963 Length 19 cm.　Width 50 cm.*

64．徐悲鴻　枇杷　紙本　1946年作　縱19厘米　橫50厘米

Xu Beihong: Loquats *Mounted on paper 1946 Length 19 cm. Width 50 cm.*

65．潘天壽　蘭石圖　紙本　1963年作　縱19厘米　橫50厘米

Pan Tianshou: Rock and Orchid *Mounted on paper 1963 Length 19 cm. Width 50 cm.*

66. 吴湖帆　墨竹　紙本　1962年作　縱19厘米　橫50厘米

Wu Hufan: Bamboo in Ink *Mounted on paper* *1962* *Length 19 cm. Width 50 cm.*

67. 徐子鶴　黄山松雲　紙本　1976 年作　縱 19 厘米　橫50厘米

Xu Zihe: Pines and Clouds on Mount Huangshan *Mounted on paper* *1976* *Length 19 cm. Width 50 cm.*

68．謝稚柳　荷塘野趣圖　紙本　1965年作　縱19厘米　橫50厘米

Xie Zhiliu: Lotus Pond　*Mounted on paper　1965　Length 19 cm. Width 50 cm.*

69．朱屺瞻　杜鵑花　紙本　1961年作　縱19厘米　橫50厘米

Zhu Qizhan: Azaleas　*Mounted on paper　1961　Length 19 cm. Width 50 cm.*

70．陳衡烙　紅梅　紙本　約1932年作　縱19厘米　橫55厘米

Chen Henglao: Red Plum Blossoms *Mounted on paper 1932*
Length 19 cm. Width 55 cm.

71．徐紹青　芙蓉臘嘴鳥　紙本　1976年作　縱19厘米　橫50厘米

Xu Shaoqing: Cottonrose and Ivory-beaked Bird *Mounted on Paper 1976*
Length 19 cm. Width 50 cm.

72．田世光　紅葉小鳥　紙本　1973年作　縱19厘米　橫50厘米

Tian Shiguang: Red Leaves and Bird *Mounted on paper 1973 Length 19 cm. Width 50 cm.*

73．張辛稼　芙蓉花　紙本　1972年作　縱19厘米　橫50厘米

Zhang Xinjia: Cottonroses *Mounted on paper 1972 Length 19 cm. Width 50 cm.*

中國畫的藝術特色

中國畫在世界美術寶庫中的價值，從來是被人們所公認的。然而他和歐洲繪畫藝術相比，有明顯的不同發展。

因爲書法和繪畫，在中國原先是一回事——中國最早的文字是象形的小圖畫，所以中國人早就肯定書畫同源的說法。又因爲書法和繪畫都同樣使用特殊的基本工具——毛筆、易滲水的宣紙以及用烟煤摻膠制成的墨。因此，中國畫和書法確實是一對孿生姊妹。

長期以來，中國人精巧地掌握毛筆的抑揚頓挫效果，形成表達各種感情的點和線，創造出中國獨有的一門藝術——書法。中國畫則在這個基礎上更充分地發揮點、線的作用。因此，線條在中國繪畫中比歐洲繪畫發揮得更加淋漓盡緻，達到高度效果。

對中國畫影響深遠的繪畫準則——五世紀的《六法論》。把“氣韵(精神)的活動”(“氣韻生動”)放在第一位；第二是“用筆的內在力量”(“骨法用筆”)；第三才是“遇着任何事物都畫得像”(“應物象形”)。即是說：中國繪畫對於“形似”是放在第三位的。首先要求的是“神韻”和“用筆”(即掌握筆觸變化的技法)。這和後期印象派以前傳統的歐洲繪畫首先要求形似，走了不同的路。

繪畫和書法同一來源，從畫家握筆的姿勢來看也就清楚。中國人寫字作畫時，執筆是先用拇指和食指捏住筆桿，然後中指幫助食指爲一方，無名指、小指和拇指在筆桿的另一方，以取得用力的均衡，使筆桿直立。這和歐洲習慣的用筆方法完全不同，因而達到中國書畫獨有的、變化多樣而富於“迫力”的各種點和線。

傳統的歐洲美術家對於中國畫家不講究陰影光暗，和不採用焦點透視，認爲是一種遺憾(例如成書於本世紀初的《Chinese Art》 by S. W. Bushell)。當然，後期印象派以後的現代歐洲繪畫則早已打破這些規律，不但吸收了東方(包括波斯、印度和中國）繪畫的散點透視，並且也絕不嚴格地採用光線陰影的烘托方法了。

中國繪畫從原始時代的彩陶飾紋開始，就附着在日用品和建築物上。一世紀前後的秦、漢時期，開始發現畫在布帛上的畫。四、五世紀就出現卷軸形式的繪畫，但那時仍以畫在壁上或屏風上的繪畫爲主，中世紀的唐、宋時期才大量發現卷軸畫。而現在流行的“條幅”、“中堂”、“長卷”、“册頁”、“扇面”等形式的繪畫，則是十一、二世紀(宋)以後的事。

中國人創造出獨特的繪畫藝術形式，把書法（題字)、詩和畫放在一幅紙上，形成互相融合的藝術品，這也是從十一、二世紀的宋代開始的。到今天，這種形式得到普遍繼承和發展。

對於歐洲繪畫藝術説來，這是它所没有的形式。

古代中國畫家，都自製從植物和礦物中提練出來的顔料。由於紙、絹的配合，這些顔色有的可以保持千年，不易退變。現代畫家已經開始用顔料廠供應的中國畫顔色。革新派的畫家，也兼用國外輸入的水彩和廣告畫顔色。

正如歐洲現代偉大畫家畢加索和馬蒂斯都並不諱言他們的作品受到中國畫影響一樣，在中國傳統繪畫的基礎上吸收和參考歐洲繪畫方法的嘗試，中國畫家中，已經有人在努力進行。由於中西文化交流的日益頻繁，這種互相切磋的活動，必然日益密切，從而在自己民族的藝術發展上，增加養料。自然，這種交流祇能是充實和豐富，而並不等於取代自己民族原有藝術形式的優點。

江蘇省國畫院副院長、山水畫家宋文治先生平日收藏許多中國現代畫家的作品。這本畫册就是選自他所藏的一部份珍品，這六十多幅作品包括了半個多世紀以來的主要畫家的創作。這些畫家大多是宋先生的畫友。

通過這本畫册，希望提供讀者以欣賞中國現代繪畫藝術的一點美的享受。

黄　苗　子

1980年10月20日

本文及“作品欣賞與畫家介紹”的作者黄苗子先生，是廣東省中山縣人，生於1913年。現任中國文學藝術界聯合會委員，中國美術家協會理事，英文版《中國文學》雜誌美術顧問，香港《美術家》雜誌編委。著作有《美術欣賞》、《畫家徐悲鴻》、《白石老人逸話》、《古美術雜記》等，他的美術論文散見於國内外報刊雜誌。

The Characteristics of Chinese Painting

The unique place Chinese painting occupies in the world's fine arts has been universally recognised. However, it has followed its own road of development which distinguishes it from European painting arts.

Chinese calligraphy and painting are traceable to the same origin, for ancient Chinese words were hieroglyphs consisting of pictures and figures of concrete objects. And, as Chinese calligraphy and Chinese ink-painting depend on the same materials — the brush, absorbing paper and ink made from soft coal soot mixed with gum, it may be said that Chinese calligraphy and painting are twins.

For ages Chinese scholars have skilfully applied the brush in such up-and-down, ebb-and-flow, and dot-and-line ways as to express various moods, feelings and spirits. The product is a unique art — calligraphy. On this foundation Chinese painting is based and from this foundation it has developed and multiplied the functions of the *lines*. Indeed, the *lines* feature Chinese painting to a much greater extent than they do European painting.

There are certain principles exercising far-reaching influence on Chinese painting. First, "lifelike spirit"; second, "inner strength of the brush"; third, "verisimilitude". The third is of the least importance in Chinese painting. Spirit comes first. The strength of the brush counts second. European painting follows a different order of importance, placing emphasis on graphic outward appearance.

The fact that Chinese painting and calligraphy have the same origin may also be seen in the way the painter and the calligrapher manoeuvre the brush. Its handle is held between the thumb and the forefinger, with the middle finger supporting the forefinger on one side and the ring and little fingers supporting the thumb on the other. The brush is in such an erect and balanced position that the painter can distribute his strength proportionally and evenly through it in whichever direction he likes, impelling his dots and lines freely and meaningfully. This way of handling the brush is different from that of the European painter.

Some European painters regret the Chinese painters' neglect of dimness and shadow, light and shade, focus and perspective. S.W. Bushell expresses this regret in his book *Chinese Art*. Of course, the impressionist school in its later period and contemporary European painters have given up their traditional methods and orientated to scattered perspective as used by Chinese, Indian and Persian painters instead of insisting on adding shading around an object to make it stand out.

Chinese painting originated from decorations on ancient Chinese painted pottery, and as time went by such decoration was extended to architectual pieces and utensils. During the Qin dynasty before the tenth century and the Han dynasty after it, pictures were discovered on cotton and silk textiles. During the fourth and fifth centuries, crude scroll painting had appeared, but most paintings were on walls and screens. In the Middle Ages, that is, in the Tang and Song dynasties, painted scrolls appeared in large numbers. Such paintings as "side-scrolls", "middle-scrolls", "long-scrolls", "leaf from an album" and "fan-coverings", which have been in vogue to this day, came into being in the eleventh and twelfth centuries.

In China there is a unique art combining calligraphy, poetry and painting all in one. This unique art form which dates back to the Song dynasty is today as widespread and popular as ever. It is something not to be found in European painting.

Ancient Chinese painters extracted pigments from plants and minerals and applied them on scrolls made of paper and silk. Such colours have lasted for a thousand years. However, modern Chinese painters use manufactured colours, and innovating painters take to imported watercolours and advertisement colours.

This album is indicative of the efforts among many contemporary Chinese painters to adopt worthy features of Western painting into Chinese painting. While cultural exchange and relative activities are daily increasing, it is appropriate that Chinese painters should absorb new ideas from abroad. Needless to say, the fine tradition of Chinese painting is never to be replaced.

This album contains works from the collection of Mr. Song Wenzhi, Vice-Director of the Academy of Chinese Painting of Jiangsu Province and a well-known landscape painter. His collection consists of a good many modern paintings. Those included in this album range over half a century. Most of the painters are Mr. Song's friends who share his artistic tastes.

We hope that this album will provide our viewers and readers with appreciation and enjoyment of Chinese painting.

Huang Miaozi

October 20, 1980

Huang Miaozi, who wrote this article and "Paintings and Painters", was born in 1913 in Zhongshan County, Guangdong Province. A committee member of the All-China Federation of Literary and Art Circles, he is concurrently a council member of the All-China Association of Fine Art Workers, an art advisor of *Chinese Literature*, a member on the editorial board of *The Artists*, a Hongkong magazine. Among his works are *Appreciation of Fine Art Works*, *Xu Beihong the Painter*, *Anecdotes of Qi Baishi* and *Miscellanea on Ancient Fine Arts*. His articles on fine arts often appear in Chinese and foreign newspapers and magazines.

作品欣賞與畫家介紹
PAINTINGS AND PAINTERS

黄 苗 子
by Huang Miaozi

封面：劍蘭　Jacket: Sword Orchid

封面畫的作者陳佩秋（1922－），是上海著名的女畫家，她是老畫家謝稚柳先生的夫人。她的作品韶秀清艷，尤長於工筆花卉，書法也極有成就。這幅《劍蘭》用筆挺勁，色彩和諧優美，配以清秀的書法和詩句，就構成風格高雅的畫面。

The painter of *Sword Orchid* on the jacket is Chen Peijiu (1922-), a resident of Shanghai. Her husband is the artist Xie Zhiliu. Adhering to the *Gong Bi* school of art, her works are realistic and delicate, clear and beautiful, especially her flowers and plants. She is good at calligraphy, too. Her *Sword Orchid* combines her painting, calligraphy and poetry.

1．荷花鴨子　Lotus and Duck

齊白石（1863－1957）這幅荷花，運用中國特有的紙、筆、顏料和傳統的大寫意技法，把池塘裏開得很茂盛的荷花和荷葉生動地表現出來。畫家以灰黑色的調子烘托出紅荷，使它十分嬌艷。通過荷葉和荷花及水和鴨子的姿態，把清風徐來的夏日池塘，表現得栩栩欲動，這是中國繪畫藝術以簡略筆墨表現對象生態的精彩之作。齊白石是舉世聞名的中國畫家。

Painter Qi Baishi (1863-1957) employed the technique of *Ta Xie Yi* (bold lines and touches of ink and wash to bring out the spirit and significance of the object drawn), using special Chinese painting brush, paper and colours. The pond seems swimming with lotus blooms and leaves. The pale and black tints bring into relief the reddish blooms — or give an illusion of them. The leaves, blooms, water and duck together create the impression of a summer breeze blowing in, showing how Chinese ink-and wash technique works wonders. Qi Baishi was well-known throughout the world.

2．蔬菜草蟲　Chinese Cabbage and Turnip

齊白石生長在湖南的農民家庭，從小當過木工，他對於農村生活有深厚感情。這幅白菜、蘿蔔和草蟲，正是農村常見的事物。齊白石用大寫意的筆調，强烈而樸素的色彩對比，構成一幅不尋常的作品。

The painter, again Qi Baishi, came of a peasant family in Hunan Province. In his teens he was apprenticed to a carpenter. He loved his village and liked life in the countryside. This picture is typical of his painting from nature. His technique consists in freehand brushwork characterised by vivid expression and broad outline. His style is simple and yet vigorous, creating artistic works both unique and amazing.

3．暮韻圖　**Idyllic Evening**

李可染（1907－）是現在中國的著名畫家。這幅畫畫一個躺在樹上吹笛的牧童和一頭恬静地卧在地上的老牛。牧童的帽子和衣服掛在樹枝上，情景是那麼閒適，好像一首夏日黄昏的田園詩。這幅畫主要是運用中國畫法的墨和水的微妙變化，和毛筆筆觸的頓挫，構成極美妙的韵律。

Painter Li Keran (1907-) ranks high among contemporary Chinese painters. A cowherd is comfortably and securely lying in the crotch of a tree, playing his flute while his old buffalo enjoys a well-deserved rest on the ground. The boy's straw hat and jacket are hanging from a twig. All is quiet and peaceful, making an idyll of a summer evening. This scene is created by the Chinese painting brush-touches here and there, contrasting dark and light shades with ink and wash.

4－5．牡丹蝴蝶
Peony and Butterfly

長卷是中國畫的一種形式，特點是適於表現廣闊的境界，裝裱起來易於保存。這幅長卷是潘天壽（1898－1971）的作品。作者利用輕重色彩的對比，形成一幅美妙勻稱的構圖，把牡丹花和蝴蝶，都畫得富有生氣。潘天壽是中國現代著名畫家，曾任浙江美術學院院長，長期住在杭州。他的作品，以用筆勁挺，色彩豐富，構圖奇妙，有深刻的中國畫傳統和書法修養著稱。

A horizontal scroll provides more room for a panoramic painting. Pan Tianshou (1898-1971) used the technique of contrasting dark and light shades to attain a balanced and beautiful composition. The peony and butterfly are both full of life and spirit. One of the best known contemporary painters of China, Pan Tianshou was Director of the Academy of Fine Arts of Zhejiang Province. He lived in Hangzhou for the better part of his life. His paintings are full of life and strength and harmonious in colouring. He excelled in calligraphy as well as traditional Chinese painting.

6．陶淵明詩意　**Tao Yanming's Poem in Painting**

傅抱石（1904－1965）這幅小畫，是表現四世紀中國大詩人陶淵明的詩句——"採菊東籬下，悠然見南山"情景的。作者善於以細緻的筆調表現古代人物，這幅畫更深刻地表達出一種抒情詩的感覺。傅抱石教授是江西人，城市貧民出身，曾留學日本，是近四十年來中國著名畫家之一。曾歷任南京大學教授、中國美術家協會副主席等職務，長期住在南京。他的作品，近年來在國外被收藏家重價收購。

"The fence offers chrysanthemums to be gathered; South Mountain is seen in the distance." Painter Fu Baoshi (1904-1965) translated this poem into a picture, using his delicate brush lines to represent the poet and his poem. Born in Jiangsi Province of a peasant family and educated in Japan, Prof. Fu taught Chinese painting at Nanjing University and was Vice-Chairman of the All-China Association of Fine Art Workers.

7．和闐裝　**Xinjiang Costume**

葉淺予(1907－)是一位以人物畫著稱的國畫家，尤以表現舞蹈見長。他運用中國毛筆的特殊功能，輕重疾徐地表現人物神態表情，衣服質感，收到美妙的效果。這幅畫描寫新疆舞蹈的姿態，造型生動，色彩凝重飄逸，表現出新疆女性的特徵。他是中國美術家協會副主席、北京中央美術學院中國畫系主任。

Painter Yie Qianyu (1907-) specialises in figure painting. He has a distinct power of wielding the Chinese brush, now swiftly and now slowly, now heavily and now lightly to create lively figures in characteristic costume. This picture shows a young woman of Xinjiang dancing entrancingly in simple costume. Yie Qianyu is a master at expressing dancing motion and mood. He is Vice-Chairman of the All-China Association of Fine Art Workers and concurrently Dean of the Department of Chinese Painting of the Beijing Central Fine Art Academy.

8．金 魚　**Goldfish**

吳作人(1908－)早年到歐洲留學，致力油畫創作，很有成就。近年從事中國繪畫，特點是具有新的意境，從傳統的筆墨技法中加以發展，不拘守成法。這幅金魚色彩和用筆雅净凝練，表現出自然界的悠閒境界。吳作人是北京中央美術學院名譽院長，中國文學藝術界聯合會副主席，中國美術家協會副主席。

Painter Wu Zhoren (1908-), who studied oil-painting in Europe, combines the strong points of Chinese painting with those of Western painting, freeing himself from any rigid rules of either. He uses the traditional Chinese ink-and-wash technique to inject a new spirit into his Western painting. This picture of goldfish demonstrates his ability to manipulate the Chinese painting brush to express the ease of fish in water. The painter is Honorary Director of the Beijing Central Fine Art Academy and concurrently Vice-Chairman of the All-China Association of Fine Art Workers.

9－10．菊蟹圖　**Chrysanthemums and Crab**

錢松喦(1892－)是江蘇的老畫家，曾當過中學教師，現在是中國美術家協會江蘇分會名譽主席，江蘇省國畫院院長。他以山水畫著稱。這幅菊蟹圖利用紅、黃兩個主調表現出秋天的明媚色彩。他用筆清秀，繼承了十五、六世紀以來細筆花卉畫的傳統。

Painter Qian Songyan (1892-) is an old master of Chinese painting of Jiangsu Province. Formerly a teacher in a middle school, he is now Honorary Chairman of the Jiangsu branch of the All-China Association of Fine Art Workers. He is famous for his landscape painting. This picture of chrysanthemums and a crab has red and yellow as the main tints, expressing the bright and delightful atmosphere of autumn. Following the Chinese traditional technique of the fifteenth and sixteenth centuries, he employs fine brushwork with attention to detail.

11．淡墨山水　**Landscape in Pale Inking**

這是名畫家李可染的一幅山水畫，以淡墨和花青作基調，表現出一種空濛景色，富有詩意。李可染的山水畫以多層次的墨色渲染，來表現山林的無限幽深見長。這幅作品用淡墨，在他的作品中是極少見的。但是，蒼勁的用筆，勻稱而富於變化的構圖，看出了作者的才華。

Painter Li Keran (1907-) uses thick inking and spotted darkness to describe a murky atmosphere, quiet and idyllic. His peculiarity is usually multiple laying on of dark shades to bring into relief the tranquil depth of mountain and wood. This picture is an exception. Here he uses firm and straight stroking and lining of his brush, simple and yet varying in composition, exhibiting his artistic talent.

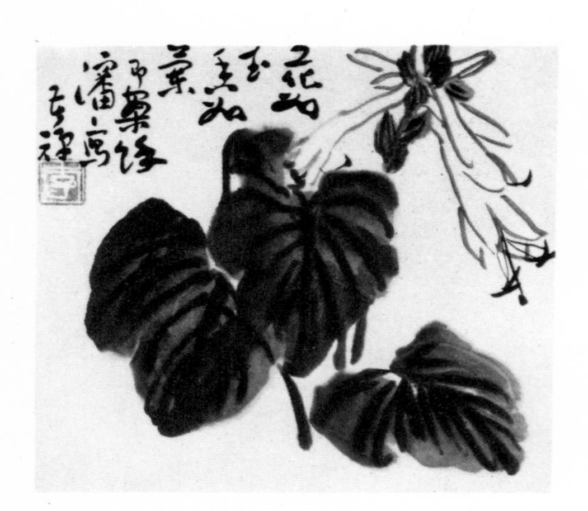

12．玉簪花　**Fragrant Plantain Lily**

玉簪花生長在墻邊或山林陰處，是一種大葉草本植物。作者用水墨和粗壯的筆調，十分簡略而傳神地抓住了花卉的生態，花的輕盈和葉的厚重都通過精練的筆法表現出來。作者李苦禪（1898－）是繼承十六世紀以來中國水墨寫意畫風的現代老畫家之一。他早年曾跟齊白石學畫。

Fragrant plantain lilies are usually found at the foot of a wall and in rock crannies. Their broad leaves give off a pleasant odour. The painter, seemingly using simply crude and simple strokes of dark ink, depicts the lively moods and spirit of flowers and plants. His technique lies in creating the lightness and mobility of flowers and the heaviness and thickness of the leaves in natural contrast. Li Kuchan, the artist (1898-), started learning Chinese painting from Qi Baishi, inheriting the traditional style of ink-and-wash for bold strokes and simple lines.

13．松鷹圖　**Pine and Hawk**

這是李苦禪的一幅水墨淡彩作品。畫上題句的意思是："老鷹盤踞在松樹上，這時正吹來了天際的風。"老鷹的嘴、眼、姿態，都畫得凶猛有神。鷹是李苦禪的作品中常畫的題材。中國畫的題字，往往和繪畫本身起着呼應的作用，構成了美妙的構圖，這幅畫就是個例子。

This picture by Li Kuchan using ink-and-wash technique and a strong contrast of black and white, conveys the idea as the inscription indicates that "the old hawk occupies the pine and is steadying himself against the wind blowing down from the skies". How fierce-looking the hawk's beak, eyes, and posture! This bird is one of the painter's favourite subjects. In Chinese painting an inscription always goes with the picture, identifying the object and mood. This work is an example.

14. 雁蕩山景 **Wild Goose Mountain**

陸儼少(1909－)是南方的山水畫名家，他的畫氣魄雄峻，筆墨蒼勁，構圖變化多樣。他繼承了十五、六世紀山水畫家石濤的風格，但發展爲自己獨特的面目。這幅浙江雁蕩山風景，用花青和淡赭石這兩種中國畫顏色爲主調，以蒼勁流利的筆觸，構成這幅感染力很强，又十分幽雅的中國畫。

Lu Yanshao (1909-) is one of the famous painters of southern China. His painting breathes the majestic strength of nature, breadth of vision and variety of composition. It inherits the style of Shi Tao, a landscape painter of the 15th-16th centuries, with some added aspects of Lu Yanshao's own. In this landscape of Wild Goose Mountain of Zhejiang Province, the painter uses spot-black and light-brown colours and firm and smooth brush-touches to create a picture full of secluded serenity amid purling brooks.

15. 絲瓜小鳥 **Snake Gourds and Bird**

唐雲(1910－)是著名的花鳥畫家，他的線條和色調輕清華麗，賦予花鳥蟲魚以活潑的生機。他發展了十六世紀以後南方花鳥畫家華嵒、虛谷等人的風格，以清新艷逸見長。這幅絲瓜小鳥圖運用對比色彩，構成和諧而有變化的調子，筆觸活潑，增加了花鳥的生氣。唐雲是上海畫院副院長。

Tang Yun (1910-) is an eminent painter of flowers and birds. His lines and colours impart life and movement to his fish and worms also. His art is a development of the styles of Hua Yan and Xu Gu, flower and bird painters who lived in south China in the 16th century. This painting of snake gourds and a bird exemplifies the technique of colours in contrast and yet in perfect natural harmony. The painter's strokes and lines describe very lifelike plants and birds.

16. 葡 萄 **Grapes**

許麟盧(1916－)畫的葡萄，筆墨縱橫馳驟，很有氣勢。他把中國書法運用到畫上(特別是右下方的葡萄藤)，這種筆觸，恰當地表現出葡萄的生機蓬勃。右上方題字，正好在構圖上起平衡變化的作用。許麟盧是齊白石的弟子。

Xu Linlu (1916-) paints from nature and life, sweeping his brush animatedly, applying calligraphic lines to painting (vide the grape vines in the lower right corner). His brush-touches bring out the vitality and fullness of grapes. His inscription at the upper right varies and balances the composition of the picture. The painter is Qi Baishi's pupil.

17．蘇州姑娘　**Suzhou Maidens**

這兩個典型的蘇州農村姑娘，她們正在洗衣和汲水的河邊相遇。這是中國畫家用傳統技法表現現代人物的作品，是作者從他的家鄉(蘇州)的生活體驗中創作出來的。調子十分朴素，線條的靈活，刻劃出南方少女的輕盈的身材。作者盧沉(1935－)是北京畫院的畫家。

Suzhou women are known for their beauty. Here, two village girls meet by a creek, one has come to wash clothes, the other to fetch water. This picture typifies the Chinese traditional technique of creating with ink-and-wash figures full of life and charm. The artist, Lu Chen, was himself born in Suzhou in 1935. An artist of the Beijing Academy of Chinese Painting, he paints from life, translating his observation of neighbours and friends into artistic images. His simple contrast of colours and his lively lines produce successful figures, especially of women of his native south.

18．雪山圖　**Snowy Mountain**

雪山圖描寫漫天大雪的北方山嶺，但衹露出山峰和峭壁，作者運用水墨和淺絳，寫出無限空闊的境界。簡練的筆觸，都是從艱苦的技法探索中出來的。作者亞明(1924－)是繼傅抱石之後的江蘇著名畫家。他從事繪畫是從他少年時代參加抗日游擊戰爭時期開始的。現在他是中國美術家協會江蘇分會主席、江蘇省國畫院副院長。

This is a mountain half buried in snow, making a precipice and its peak especially majestic and awe-inspiring. This landscape, a creation of nothing but ink-and-wash and simple lines, embodies great nature in miniature. The painter's fine and bold brush-touches speak for his painstaking technical practice. Ya Ming (1924-　) is an artist after Fu Baoshi, the famous painter of Jiangsu. Ya Ming, a guerilla fighter in the War of Resistance Against Japan, began traditional painting in his free moments. He is now Chairman of the Jiangsu branch of the All-China Association of Fine Art Workers, and Vice-Director of the Academy of Chinese Painting of Jiangsu Province.

19．柳蔭雙鳥　**Two Birds in the Shade of Willows**

林風眠(1900－)是現代中國的繪畫大師之一，是傳統國畫中革新派的倡導者。早年曾留學法國，早在三十年代就開始中國畫的創作，他的作品具有鮮明的時代感。他把歐洲現代繪畫的特點，與中國畫成功地結合起來。這幅"柳蔭雙鳥"的色彩和構圖，像輕音樂那樣給人以藝術享受。

Lin Fengmian (1900-　), a contemporary master of Chinese painting, enjoys the reputation of advocating innovation in the traditional painting style. In his student days in Paris he learned Western painting. Then in the thirties, after returning to China, he began producing Chinese paintings of a new type, infusing into them a refreshing spirit of the new times by combining the merits of Western and Chinese traditional painting. This picture of two birds in the shade of willows has an almost musical quality in its composition and tints.

20. 秋園小景 **Garden in Autumn**

運用中國畫特有的筆觸，和紅、綠、黑這些對比色彩，構成一幅秋天園野的小景，表現這種意境和情調，是中國畫的特長。這種花鳥畫的風格，不同於齊白石（如圖 1 ）那種大寫意，而是介乎工筆與寫意之間的。這種風格從十五世紀後才開始流行。作者江寒汀（1903－1963）是上海畫院的花鳥畫家。

The Chinese painting brush can be wielded in varying techniques: in rapid sweep, slow motion, in light touches, heavy strokes — and by contrasting colours: red, green, black and delicate coloration. *Garden in Autumn* demonstrates the manipulation of the Chinese painting brush by the artist. Chinese painting usually expresses ideas and feelings as they flow from the human mind. This treatment of flowers and birds is different from that of Qi Baishi (vide picture 1). Jiang Handing (1903-1963) places his technique somewhere between the traditional and modern arts. Jiang was a flower-and-bird painter on the faculty of the Shanghai Academy of Chinese Painting.

21－22. 牡丹蝴蝶

Peony and Butterfly

陳佩秋這幅牡丹蝴蝶長卷，色彩明艷，栩栩如生，十分動人。牡丹的紫色和蝴蝶後翅的紅色遙相呼應。牡丹的姿態十分輕盈，它和蝴蝶以及寫得十分瀟灑的題字，構成了勻稱而有變化的構圖。這是女畫家獨有的艷逸細緻的風格。

This horizontal scroll by Chen Peiqiu is brilliant and lively. The purple peony and the red legs of the butterfly are successfully complementary. Peony, butterfly and inscription form an art entity peculiarly Chinese. The work is a great credit to this outstanding woman painter.

23. 青　蛙 **Frog on Rock**

這是一幅小册頁，作於1974年。這幅畫和陳佩秋前兩幅作品（護封面及21圖）純粹的工筆畫不同，這一幅的青蛙用工筆，而石頭則用寫意筆調。這不但沒有不調和的感覺，反而突出了青蛙這個主題。

Chen Peiqiu painted this frog in 1974 — a slight departure from the fine bruswork with attention to detail (*Gong Bi* technique) seen in the picture on the jacket of this album and in picture 21 above. The uniqueness of this picture lies in the contrast of the artist's fine hand in doing the frog and freehand for the rock.

24．鍾馗小妹圖 **Zhong Kui and His Sister**

程十髮(1921－)這幅作品，畫的是一位中國古代傳說中的神仙── 鍾馗和他的妹妹在舊歷五月初五這個端陽節日裏，敲着歌板吹蕭慶樂的情景。鍾馗是一個專替人間捉鬼的可愛的仙人，許多畫家和戲劇家都以他爲題材從事藝術創作。作者程十髮是一位多能的上海畫家，他的人物畫得到國内外人士的喜愛。

Cheng Shifa (1921-) gives vividness to the legendary figure and his younger sister celebrating the Dragon Boat Festival, brother playing the castanets, sister the flute. The fairy is loved by the folk around for his feats in catching ghosts, and he is a favourite hero for painters and playwrights. Cheng Shifa is a versatile painter of Shanghai, popular among Chinese and foreign friends.

25．犛牛圖 **Yaks**

犛牛是中國西南部高原的動物,西藏人把牠養起來作爲載運力役之用。犛牛毛長，硬壯有力。吴作人在四十年代初旅行青康高原回來後，就喜歡以犛牛爲題材。這幅畫以濃墨和淡墨表現兩種毛色的犛牛，筆觸簡練，但充分地表現出力量。

The yak is a draught animal found in Tibet, long-haired and strong. Wu Zhoren took to the Yak as the object of his art after his tour of Tibet in the forties. This picture is a product of thick and thin ink-and-wash. Wu's brush-touches are bold and vigorous.

26. 松枝黄花 **Pine Needles and Day Lilies**

這是以一種黄花的野生植物及松枝爲題材的花卉畫。作者利用重色的枝幹和淺色的松枝作對比，使構圖筆觸都達到了美妙的預想。作者鄧林是北京畫院一位年輕的女畫家。

Deng Lin, a woman painter of flowers and plants, uses in this picture the contrasting black and pale ink-and-wash touches to paint from nature. She is a young artist of the Beijing Academy of Chinese Painting.

27. 墨 松 **Pine**

吴湖帆(1894－1968)是居住上海的著名畫家,他的風格以淡雅清逸見長。他繼承了十四、五世紀他的同鄉文徵明 、唐寅這些“蘇州派”(又稱“吴門派”)畫風。這幅水墨松樹用筆清秀婉約,代表他的風格。吴湖帆是位學者、詩人、畫家，世代收藏書畫。

Wu Hufan (1894-1968) of Shanghai paints in a style that consists of the simplicity, delicacy and lucidity of the Suzhou School, popularised by Wen Zhenming and Tang Yin of the 15th and 16th centuries. *Pine* typifies this technique. Besides painting, Wu was a poet, scholar and collector of paintings.

28. 紅 梅 **Red Plum Blossoms**

梅花是中國畫家喜愛的題材，從十世紀以來就有許多畫家專畫梅花。這幅《紅梅》是畫家關山月的手筆，以紅、黑兩色爲基調，枝幹縱横有力，構圖也不一般。關山月(1912－)是廣東的名畫家，他是中國美術家協會廣東分會的主席。

Chinese painters have been fond of red plum blossoms as the theme of their artistic creation since the 10th century. Guang Shanyue (1912-), who used this theme here, contrasts red and black in his technique, employing bold ink strokes for trunk and branches and delicate red colouring to touch out the blooms. Well-known as a painter of Guangdong Province, he holds the post of Chairman of the Guangdong branch of the All-China Association of Fine Art Workers.

29－30. 川江險水圖 **Treacherous Waters of a Sichuan River**

這是從前未經治理的長江四川一段風景，水勢湍急，波濤洶湧，來往船隻十分危險。作者陸儼少通過深刻的觀察和感受，用淋漓筆墨繪出波紋、浪花和驚濤，在向大自然博鬪中前進的小船，屹立在江邊的懸崖斷岸，構成一首壯瀾的史詩。作者在畫旁題道，留下這個景色是爲了告訴未來的人，整頓山河建設國家是艱苦的事業。

Until recently untamed, this section of the Yangzi River in Sichuan Province used to strike fear into the hearts of voyagers as the rapids and torrents threatened the safety of all vessels sailing upstream or downstream. Through his meticulous observation, deep impression and keen feeling, Lu Yanshao (1909-) employs ink-and-wash to create ripples, spray and torrential waters. Small boats are tossed about as they push against the raging waters, with crags and precipices looking down. This picture is poetic in its majestic implications. And the painter adds to its poetry this inscription: “Let posterity know that taming the River (Yangzi) is a herculean task they are to take up.”

31．春　艷　**Spring Beauty**

這是描繪栽在盆上的兩朵牡丹花。牡丹的紅、白色和緑葉相映十分鮮艷，花和葉都用線條勾出輪廓，線條都十分遒勁。但花和葉的勾法不同，以顯出不同的質感。作者鄭乃珖（1912－）福建人，曾在陝西西安美術學院任教。他是花鳥畫的專家。

There stand in the pot two peomes, one red and the other white, and the leaves are green. The three colours set off one another to advantage. The flowers and leaves are formed with clearcut and distinctive lines, but the technique of drawing the lines of the flowers is different from that of drawing the leaves, producing also a different effect. Zheng Naiguang (1921-), a native of Fujian, excells in flower-and-bird painting. He has taught at the Academy of Fine Arts of Sian.

32．松鼠山楂　**Squirrel and Hawthorns**

來楚生（1902－1975）是上海的花鳥畫家。他善於捕捉動物的神態，這幅松鼠捧着山楂吃的神氣就是一個好例子。這幅畫用簡潔的紅黑對比，產生良好的韵律。題字、松鼠和菓子的梯形構圖，更顯得錯落有緻。

Lai Chusheng (1902-1975) also specialised in flowers and birds but was quick to catch the posture and spirit of animals. Here a squirrel nibbles at a hawthorn. Lai's technique, as demonstrated in this picture, is red-and-black contrast with harmony. The squirrel, the hawthorns and the inscription combine to make a vivid picture.

33．獻花舞　**Flower Dance**

葉淺予這幅描寫印度舞蹈——獻花舞的作品是他愛畫的題材之一。這幅1977年的作品筆觸老練，準確地掌握了美妙的舞姿。色彩也更加沉靜和諧，充分發揮了中國畫線條和色彩的特長，使畫面富有東方情調。

Yie Qianyu depicts an Indian girl dancing as she offers a wreath at a religious ceremony. It typifies Yie's favourite artistic theme. This work was produced in 1977 and shows the painter quite at home with his ink-and-wash touches capable of etching out delicate dancing steps and figures. Yie's lines and tints are quiet and harmonious, suiting the oriental atmosphere.

34．深山幽谷圖　Mountain and Gully

魏紫熙(1915－)是南京畫派的畫家，他的風格和傅抱石、亞明接近。這幅畫描寫跨過兩山石澗的一棵樹，猴子在樹上樹下活動，逼真地寫出深山幽谷的清寂境界，意境極美。畫中的坡樹和山澗，一濃一淡，有虛實相生之妙。

Wei Zixi (1915-) is a painter of the Nanjing School, his style being close to those of Fu Baoshı and Ya Ming. The old tree in this picture bends over the gully like a bridge spanning the opposite hills. Monkeys frisk on the bank and on the tree branch. The painter's ink-and-wash technique produces a vivid scene in a secluded mountain gully. The dark tree against the whiteness of the gully is a contrast of tints from the Chinese painting brush.

35．扁豆蟋蟀圖　Catalpa Pods and Crickets

陳大羽(1912－)是南京畫家，他以畫公鷄見稱。這幅扁豆蟋蟀圖，用中國草書的筆法畫豆藤，十分飛舞有勁，紫色的豆莢用花青色葉子襯出，格外明媚。左下角兩個蟋蟀，筆墨生動。這是寫意花卉小品的佳作。

Chen Dayu (1912-), a painter of Nanjing well-known for his roosters, here takes another theme. Though an exception, it is a success, its remarkable feature being that the vines are derived from running and cursive Chinese calligraphic lines—sweeping and vigorous. The purple bean pods lie attractively against the background of the green leaves. The two crickets are full of life. This picture typifies the technique of painting flowers and plants by freehand brushwork characterised by vivid expression and bold outline.

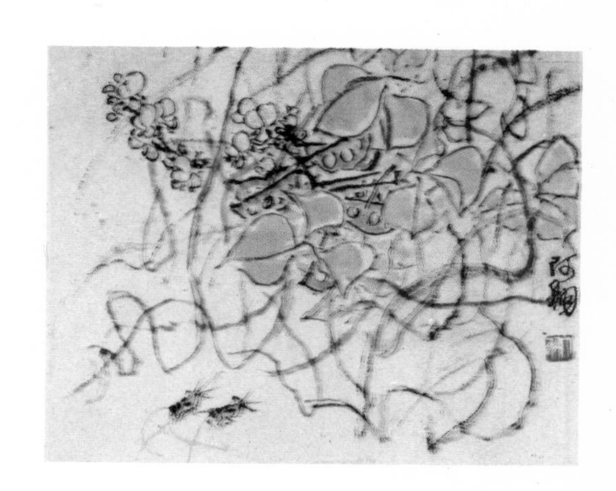

36．紅山茶　Red Camellias

羅叔子(1913－1968)是南京的畫家、工藝美術史及美術史家，生前在南京藝術師範學院教書，他晚年遭到不幸，死時比較年輕。

羅叔子這幅《紅山茶》用重色畫葉，襯出紅花，情調幽雅清艷，花葉和枝幹疏密相間，與題字結合，形成美妙的構圖。

Luo Shuzi (1913-1968) was a painter of Nanjing, versed in industrial arts history and fine arts. He was an art instructor at the Teachers' College of Arts of Nanjing. Unfortunately, he did not live to a ripe old age. In painting this picture he used heavy colouring for the leaves to set off the red flowers, providing aesthetic qualities for enjoyment. His composition is a harmonious and pleasing interposition of leaves, flowers and a poetic inscription.

37. 駱　駝　**Camel**

黃冑（1925－）是一位意志堅强，努力不息的畫家。他因從軍曾在新疆住過，所以畫過很多新疆風物，這幅《駱駝》就是他描寫新疆的題材之一。黃冑的用筆豪放矯健，不受傳統技法的拘束而帶着速寫情調。這幅作品也看出他的本來面目。

Huang Zhou (1925-　) is a painter distinguished by a strong will and painstaking work. His experience as a soldier in Xinjiang has given him images of local colour, which he has translated into impressive pictures in the traditional Chinese ink-and-wash style. The camel is reminiscent of Xinjiang. Huang Zhou's brushwork is free from any rigidity in the traditional style but adheres to its broad and bold sweep.

38. 令箭荷花　**Cactus Bloom**

令箭荷花是仙人掌科的一種。王雪濤（1903－）這位著名的北方老畫家，用他熟練的筆觸，概豁地把它的欣欣生意表現出來。令箭荷花和梗的質感，蝴蝶的動態，都十分傳神。全幅畫没有任何一筆是多餘的，看出畫家的功力之深。

Wang Xuetao (1903-　) is a well-known painter of the north. His expert brushwork enables him to bring out a vivid and lively depiction of an object with a few touches and strokes. The cactus bloom and stem give an impression of beauty and sturdiness, while the butterflies furnish a charming foil. Not a line or touch is superfluous, a remarkable feature of the painter's work.

39. 黃魚蛤蜊　**Croaker and Clams**

張大壯（1903－1980）是上海老畫家，他以花鳥畫見長。這幅黃花魚和蛤蜊，描寫南方人通常喜食的水産。黃花魚用輕快的筆觸，幾筆就鈎出了魚的形態，蛤蜊也衹是寥寥幾筆，就産生了形神兼備的效果。優秀的中國畫，常常具有這種特點。

Zhang Dazhuang (1903-1980) is famous for his flowers and birds. Sparing of brushwork, he made a few strokes and touches to bring out the forms and atmosphere of the picture. In fact, such economy and vividness characterise Chinese painting.

40．陝北一景　**Scene in North Shanxi Province**

這位陝西的杰出畫家石魯(1911－)，近三十年來才開始創作中國畫，他以構思奇妙，氣勢非凡見稱。他的作品不同於一般的中國畫。這幅山水描寫陝西北部的牧民在山谷間牧羊的景色。因爲山上羊群一片白色，所以題句是"疑是白雲飛"。這幅畫的山勢，筆調雄壯，陝北的紅土和羊群的白色，用硃砂色填空技法作出巧妙對比。

Shi Lu (1911-) of North Shanxi started painting about thirty years ago and is known especially now for his mountains-and-water works. His composition is extraordinary; his picturesque scene unique and imposing. The white dots represent woolly lambs climbing the slope,while the shepherd sits on the edge of a crag enjoying his leisure and quiet nature around him. The inscription asks: "Are they lambs or clouds?" The question points to the delicacy and yet vigour of the painter's brushwork. The red earth and white lambs accentuate the contrast of tints.

41．黄山清凉台　**Cool Mount Huangshan**

應野平(1910－)是上海畫院的山水畫家。這幅黄山風景，在傳統的中國山水畫中，參以西洋繪畫的光暗原理，用深沉調子反襯出山的受光部分，這是現代畫家在中國畫中參以西法的例子。

Ying Yieping (1910-) is a landscape painter of the Shanghai Academy of Chinese Painting. This picture of Mount Huangshan speaks for his skilful blending of the Chinese ink-and-wash technique and Western alternate dark and light shading. The light tint visualises the sunny mountain valley, showing the complementary functions of Chinese and Western painting techniques.

42．石　榴　**Pomegranates**

王个簃(1897－)是以中國書法的用筆來作畫的寫意派花鳥畫家，他是中國現代重要畫家吴昌碩(1844－1927)的弟子。這幅石榴用筆老練豪放，書法藝術的味道很濃厚，這需要畫家有豐富的藝術修養和長期的書畫技法鍛煉才做得到的。

Wang Geyi (1897-) applied the stroking technique of Chinese calligraphy to the painting of flowers and birds, that is, painting from image. He studied with the old master Wu Changshi (1844-1927). The technique exhibited in this picture consists in the painter's freehand brushwork characterised by vivid expression and bold outline, a result of his long-time study and persistent practice.

43. 新疆哈薩克族婦女　**Xinjiang Woman**

這是一幅新疆婦女的坐像，臉型首先刻劃出中國哈薩克族婦女的特徵。衣服用筆放縱，利用適當的水墨渲染表現裙子的質感十分成功。作者周思聰（1939－）是位有才華的年青女畫家，她是中國美術家協會北京分會的副主席。

Here is a Kazak woman in sitting posture, her facial features characteristic of her nationality. Her costume represents the technique of ink-and-wash for bold outline and vivid expression. Zhou Sichong (1939-), a young and talented woman painter, is Vice-Chairman of the Beijing branch of the All-China Association of Fine Art Workers.

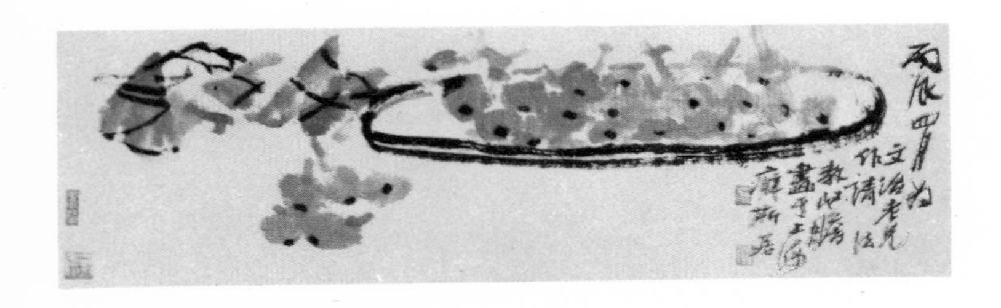

44. 枇杷粽子
Loquats and *Zongzi*

這幅長卷畫的是枇杷和粽子，粽子是用麻竹葉或粽葉蘆葉和草繩裏着糯米的食物。據古代傳說，人民因公元前四世紀的偉大詩人屈原投江自殺，把粽子投到江裏來祭祀他的（一説是爲了怕蛟龍吃屈原的尸體，用粽子來喂蛟龍）。這幅長卷以盛滿枇杷的盤占主要畫面，粽子放在左上方，題字在右面，構成勻稱的布局。作品用筆老辣，色彩簡單明艷。

Zongzi is a sweet glutinous rice dumpling wrapped in a bamboo leaf. Legend has it that after the great poet Qu Yuan of the 4th century B.C. drowned himself in a river, the people who loved him made *zongzi* in large quantities and threw them into the waters to feed the dragon, the controller of the river, so that he would not eat the poet. This picture in the ink-and-wash brushwork of Zhu Qizhan (1892-) shows a plateful of loquats with a few *zongzi* by the side.

45. 枇杷拳石　**Loquats and Rock**

這幅《枇杷拳石》和上一幅《枇杷粽子》都是朱屺瞻（1892－）的作品。朱屺瞻是上海的老畫家，他先是在日本和法國學油畫，風格接近於Henri Matisse，晚年專致力於中國畫。這幅册頁具有鮮明的現代色彩感，筆觸則純粹是中國風格。

Again the loquats of Zhu Qizhan, this time with a rock. The artist studied painting in Japan and France, his style being close to that of Henri Matisse. In his later years now, he devotes himself to Chinese traditional painting, of which this picture is an example.

46. 芙蓉花和蟹 **Cottonrose and Crab**

陳子奮(1897－1976)是福建花鳥畫家，他以雙鈎（用毛筆細線準確地畫出花鳥輪廓）筆法見長。這幅芙蓉花和蟹，是雙鈎細筆，芙蓉花的老幹，却用粗筆寫意，並且巧妙地用題字來處理構圖以及粗細筆之間的矛盾，使畫面發生和諧感。

Chen Zifen (1897-1976) of Fujian specialised in flowers and birds, using fine outlines to bring into relief his flowers, as illustrated in this picture. The thick branch of the tree in contrast is a piece of brushwork characterised by vivid expression and bold outline.

47. 玉簪花 **Fragrant Plantain Lilies**

此畫和圖12都是玉簪花，這幅接近於白描筆法，而圖12則採用水墨的渲染。由於作者熟練地掌握中國毛筆技巧，所以鈎線舒適自如，刻畫了玉簪花葉的神態。作者賀天健(1890－1977)是上海老畫家，尤以山水畫見長。曾經寫過一本他畫山水畫的心得，受到美術界的重視。

The technique used in this picture is mainly simple and plain lines, while thePlantain Liliesin picture 12 are produced by ink-and-wash. The painter simply but skilfully employed the Chinese painting brush to lay down a few lines describing leaves quite true to life. The painter, He Tianjian (1890-1977), was a fine painter of landscapes, which he collected into an album highly valued by fine art workers.

48. 墨　梅 **Plum Blossoms**

錢瘦鐵(1896－1967)是上海的老畫家，曾久住日本。他的畫以清逸高雅見長。這幅水墨梅花，正是他自己的風格。中國畫家經常把梅花的清香淡素，比做具有清高品質的人而加以歌頌。

Qian Shoutie (1896-1967) was a Shanghai painter who resided in Japan for many years. His plum blossoms done in ink-and-wash appear clean, tranquil, elegant and noble — qualities generally ascribed to Chinese scholars.

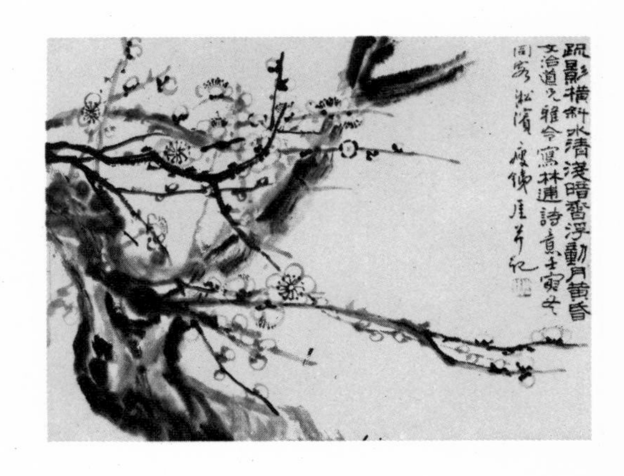

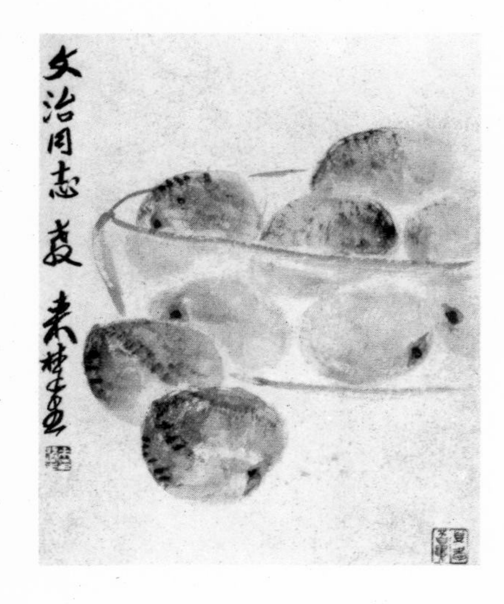

49．水蜜桃 **Honey Peaches**

來楚生的這一幅小品，畫玻璃缸裏放着的水蜜桃。古代中國畫没有人畫過玻璃缸，這是作者運用傳統中國畫技法來表現新事物的可喜嘗試，用烘托的手法，畫出玻璃的質感，十分成功。

Lai Chusheng was the first to depict glassware in traditional painting, a breakthrough that was a success. Its merit lay in the traditional Chinese ink-and-wash technique that he used, creating a glass fruit-holder which contrasted in shading with the peaches it contained.

50．白 鷺 **Egret**

林風眠的這幅《白鷺》是作者喜愛的題材，伸張着雙翅的白鷺神態閒適，筆觸和線條富有韵律感。林風眠成功地把現代色彩感覺移植入中國繪畫領域之中，象一首清新的抒情詩。這幅《白鷺》代表了他的風格。

The egret is one of Lin Fengmian's favourite themes. With wings spread as it walks in dignified and quick steps, the bird is a creation of delicate slender lines and ink touches, while rhythm pervades the whole picture. The painter injects the traditional Chinese painting with Western impressive white colouring. The egret in its setting forms a poem-in-painting, doing justice to the artist's style.

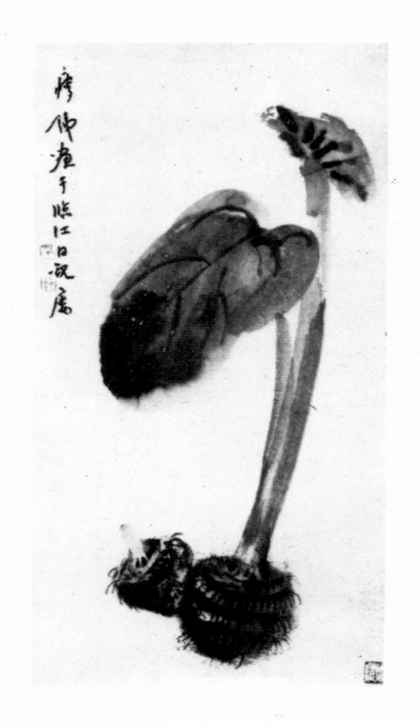

51．墨芋圖 **Taro**

芋是中國南方的植物，梗下是球形的塊莖，可以煮食。這幅墨芋圖用淡素的筆墨，表現出含有生命的植物姿態，構圖也十分匀稱。錢瘦鐵是善於通過筆墨，表現出一種清逸的感情的。

Taro is grown for food in China's southern provinces. This picture in ink-and-wash technique by Qian Shoutie gives vivid expression to plant life, as does his *Plum Blossoms,* above.

52．水仙花 **Narcissus**

綽約多姿的水仙花，從中世紀以來就常常被中國畫家採入畫中。這幅畫用冷色調表現水仙的性格，以堅硬的石頭和柔媚多姿的水仙作對比，筆觸更是揮灑自如。謝稚柳（1910－）是山水花鳥都精通的老畫家，他的作品富有韵味。他又是一位研究古書畫的學者，現任上海畫院副院長。

The narcissus, pure, elegant and fragrant, has been a favourite subject of Chinese paintings since ancient times. The Chinese simple and light tints suit the character of the narcissus to perfection, and the background of the hard rock sets off the delicate flower beautifully. The brushwork of Xie-Zhiliu (1910-) sweeps where strength is needed, touches where the requirement is softness. His flowers and birds are thus lively and rhythmic. The painter is a calligrapher as well. He is Vice-Director of the Shanghai Academy of Chinese Painting.

53－54．金 魚 **Goldfish**

金魚是近代花鳥畫家愛畫的題材。唐雲這幅畫畫出四尾在水中優悠自得的金魚。他通過植物動蕩的倒影來表現金魚是在水中，却没有畫一筆水。中國繪畫常常用烘托的手法，巧妙地表現環境而不用實景的描寫。這幅作品通過筆觸、色調，把柔和輕快的情調感染給欣賞者。

Goldfish rank high among the themes of contemporary Chinese painters. Four goldfish appear to be swimming among reeds, which in turn seem to be moving in water. All is illusion created by the technique of contrast in traditional Chinese painting: something appears to be so which is not. Tang Yun's light touches and tints give a sensation of soft and delightful rhythm.

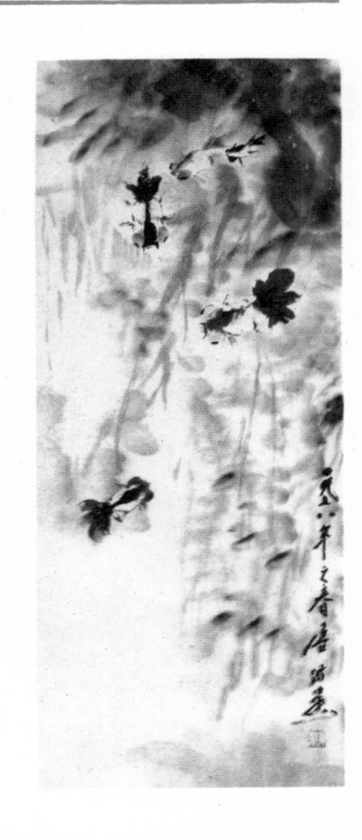

55．花 卉 **Flowers**

關良（1899－）也是一位吸收歐洲現代流派的中國畫家。他曾留學日本，以繪畫中國戲劇題材的作品著名。這幅花卉正是以中國畫方式融合歐洲現代畫風的作品。

Guang Liang (1899-) was the first among Chinese painters to assimilate merits of Western painting after studying in Japan. His paintings relating to classical drama are famous. *Flowers* is a composite of the artist's Chinese and Western arts.

56. 葡萄臘嘴 **Grapes and Ivory-beaked Birds**

羅叔子的這幅花鳥畫，與前幅(圖36《紅山茶》)風格不同，説明畫家在各種技法上進行艱苦探索。這一幅畫用寫意方法描寫秋風中的葡萄和臘嘴鳥，意境甚高。畫家没法畫風，但通過鳥群的瑟縮，葡萄的搖拽這些動態，秋風的感覺就表現出來。這是中國畫的特點之一。

This picture by Luo Shuzi (different in technique from picture 36) is a product of freehand brushwork characterised by vivid expression and bold outline: five birds perching on a grape vine, trembling in the autumn wind. That the birds are cold is shown by their tucking in their beaks and pressing closely against one another.

57. 群驢圖 **Donkeys**

黄胄最喜愛的題材是驢子，他畫過千百幅驢，他對於驢子的動態、性格都有深刻的觀察和表現能力。中國畫家主張"神似"，主張"以形寫神"。這幅在柳樹下的三匹驢子，通過水墨的變化自如，栩栩如生地描繪出驢子的特點和神態。

The painter Huang Zhou is noted for his fondness for donkeys and has given us several hundred of these attractive animals on paper. His sharp observation of donkeys' movements, habits and temperament enable his rendering of them to satisfy the criteria of "spiritual verisimilitude" and "characterisation through form and appearance". These three donkeys beneath willow branches, appearing impressively alive, are a product of traditional Chinese ink-and-wash painting.

58. 雄鷄牽牛花 **Cock and Morning Glories**

王雪濤這幅雄鷄和牽牛花圖，筆觸十分老練，雄鷄的姿態栩栩如生，這種近於寫意的筆調，從十五世紀明代開始，直至十九世紀末都是比較流行的花鳥畫派之一。他以捕捉對象的瞬間神態見長。

Wang Xuetao's rooster and morning glories, breathing the activity and freshness of dawn, represent an art akin to freehand brushwork characterised by vivid expressionate bold outline. This theme was popular from the Ming dynasty in the 15th century to the end of the 19th century. The painter was keen in catching a rooster's instantaneous typical movement and mood.

59. 猫 **Cat**

張正宇(1903－1976)是一位多面發展的藝術家，他在漫畫、裝飾畫、舞台設計和書法方面都有貢獻。這幅天真活潑的小猫畫像，利用宣紙和水墨的性能，充分表現猫身上茸毛的質感。

Zhang Zhengyu (1903-1976) was a versatile artist who was good at caricature, decorative painting and stage designing. This little cat is done on *Xuan* paper*, using ink-and-wash technique.

* *See "Paper" under the section on Chinese painting tools, p.109 of this album.*

60. 茶花雙鳥 **Camellias and Two Birds**

程十髮是人物畫家，又是花鳥畫家，這一幅用没骨的方法畫兩朵紅茶花，小鳥的神態也很生動。畫的特點是用筆流利，色彩鮮艷。

Cheng Shifa is a painter of flowers and birds as well as of figures. The two red camellias are done by brush-touches without an outline (*Mo Go*). The birds are lifelike. The success of this painting is due to the swift application of the Chinese painting brush and bright co-ordination of tints.

扇面上的繪畫 **Paintings on Fan-coverings**

61. 紫藤蜜蜂 **Wistaria and Bees**

中國文人的扇子，多由名家繪制書畫，這些扇面用過後裝裱起來，就成爲一種規格特殊的作品。

這幅紫藤蜜蜂是齊白石描寫北京春天庭院裏常見的景物，紫藤嬌艷如生，蜜蜂的雙翅急速搧動。藤蘿迎風摇蕩，看得出中國寫意畫的特點。

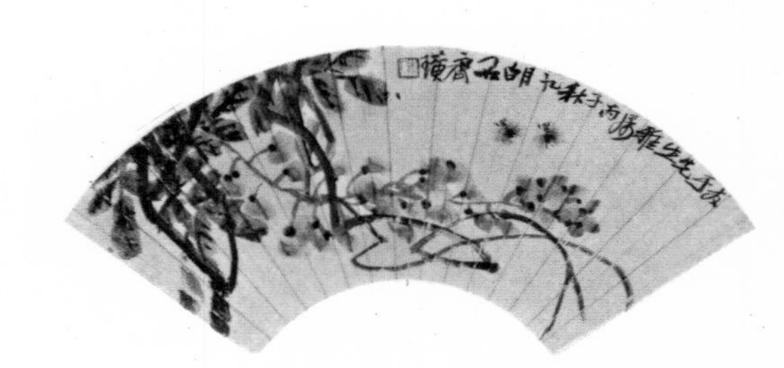

Chinese scholars adorn their fans with calligraphy and painting. When the fan is worn out and before it is discarded, the inscribed or painted covering is removed and mounted and so becomes an object of art in its own right. This fan covering by Qi Baishi depicts spring coming to the courtyard of a house in Beijing and being welcomed by wistaria with bees flitting about the flowers. The Chinese painting style of free and bold brushwork can be seen and appreciated here.

62. 山　水　**Landscape**

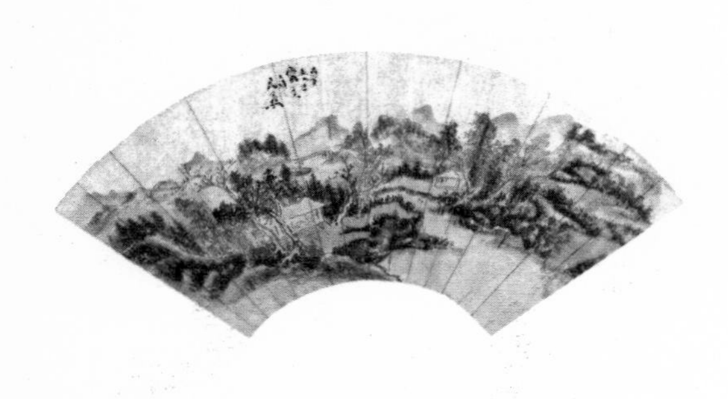

黃賓虹（1865－1955）是安徽人，晚年久住杭州，是和齊白石齊名的重要畫家。他的山水有深厚的傳統基礎，中年以後，一再變革，晚年在濃墨中施重彩，形成意境深邃的山水風格。這幅是中年後的作品，氣韵渾成淡遠，看出作者的功力。

Painter Huang Binhong (1863-1955), a native of Anhwei Province, was comtemporary with and as famous as Qi Baishi. In his later years he lived in Hangzhou, a place of charming scenery. His landscapes are based on traditional painting. In middle age, he built on the traditional foundation with innovations, while later he applied heavy inking for strong colouring and so established an important style in landscape painting. This scene speaks of his striving forward after middle age, signifying his spirit of harmony and his quiet and penetrating vision.

63. 行吟圖　**Poet Reciting as He Strolls**

傅抱石《行吟圖》扇面，近景是松樹，遠景是個行吟的詩人。這幅畫境界很高，布局新奇，人物雖小但神態高逸，松樹隨意塗染而生意葱郁。這種奇特的構圖使小幅的畫面展開寬廓的天地。

Painter Fu Baoshi gives us a periscopic view of pines in the near distance and a scholar reciting a poem as he walks. The layout of the scene is clear-cut and novel. The figure of the poet stands out in the natural world, independent, free, noble. The pines, as if daubed at will by the painter, are amply luxuriant, lively and vigorous. This unique composition unfolds in the limited space of a fan-covering heaven, earth and man in perfect harmony.

64. 枇　杷　**Loquats**

這是徐悲鴻（1895－1953）所畫的扇面。一株枇杷，葉用水墨，枇杷用植物顏色的黃色，構成和諧的調子，構圖亦錯落有緻。徐悲鴻曾在法國留學，擅長油畫，創作以歷史故事爲題材的大幅油畫和中國畫，是世界知名的畫家。他逝世後在北京爲他設立了徐悲鴻紀念館。

Xu Beihong (1895-1953) drew with a few bold ink strokes the leaves on the stem from which hangs a cluster of loquats, yellowish in colour. The composition has harmony. The painter who studied oil-painting in France, created sizable scrolls in oil depicting historical tales. His paintings in Chinese ink-and-wash earned him lasting fame. There is a Xu Beihong Memorial Hall in Beijing with a gallery attached.

65. 蘭石圖　**Rock and Orchid**

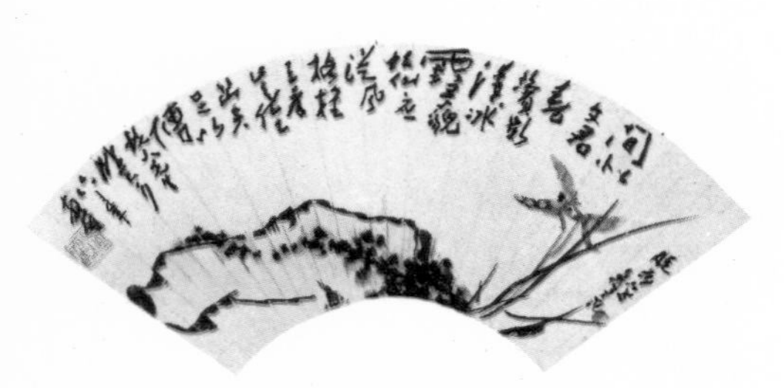

這幅蘭花石頭扇面，是詩、書、畫結合成的一個藝術整體，使欣賞的人得到更多藝術享受的一個例子。歌頌蘭花的詩句與下方的畫互相呼應形成美妙的構圖的書法，以及挺拔剛勁的蘭石，恰到好處地配合起來，構成這件美妙的藝術品。這是潘天壽這位現代重要畫家擅長的手法。

This is another tri-art work, composed of painting, calligraphy and poetry, and bringing the enjoyment of all at once. The painter's poem, in his calligraphy, is an ode to the orchid. His composition depicting the flower and rock shows elegance and strength. It is one of the best works of the contemporary painter Pan Tianshou.

66. 墨 竹 **Bamboo in Ink**

中國畫家把他們愛畫的題材：梅、蘭、竹、菊稱爲“四君子”，竹比喻爲虛心而有節操的人。這幅墨竹扇面是吴湖帆的作品，用筆秀逸，從書法出來。

The plum blossom, orchid, bamboo and chrysanthemum were the "four gentlemen" of traditional Chinese painters. Bamboo symbolised men of humbleness and strong morality. This fan-covering picturing bamboo was done by the painter Wu Hufan, whose works are characterised by simplicity, elegance and strength — derived, it is believed, from his calligraphy.

67. 黄山松雲 **Pines and Clouds on Mount Huangshan**

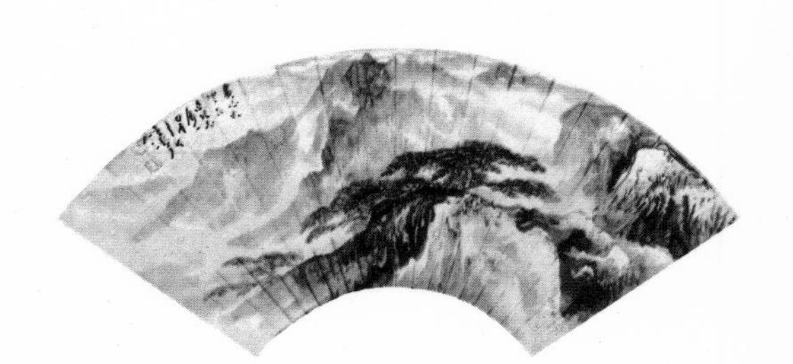

黄山是中國安徽省的一處名勝，十七世紀以來，許多山水畫家愛畫黄山，不但因爲山嶺和松樹的奇絶，更主要是黄山的雲，使山容千變萬化。這幅扇面是畫家徐子鶴的作品，他以皴染的方法表現烟雲出沒的黄山很爲成功。

Mount Huangshan in Anhui Province is one of China's scenic areas which has been a favourite subject for landscape painters since the 17th century. Its attraction has been not only the crags and pines, which are strangely beautiful and majestic, but its clouds, ephemeral and turning the mountain into a panorama of kaleidoscopic changes. This painting by Xu Zihe demonstrates his technique of showing crags and the texture of rocks and mountains by light ink touches and the use of shading and tinting to set off every aspect of the scene to advantage.

68. 荷塘野趣圖 **Lotus Pond**

這幅《荷塘野趣圖》是謝稚柳的作品，荷花荷葉紅緑相間，加上一只黑白色小鳥，艷麗和清雅的色彩構成和諧的畫面。謝稚柳是以善於吸取中世紀宋代畫院風格著稱的。這幅扇面，在色彩上很接近於宋畫。

The lotus flowers and leaves complement one another nicely, while a black and white bird perched on a lotus stem appears quite at home among the green and pink of the plant. The painter Xie Zhiliu borrows his technique from old masters of the Song dynasty.

69. 杜鵑花 **Azaleas**

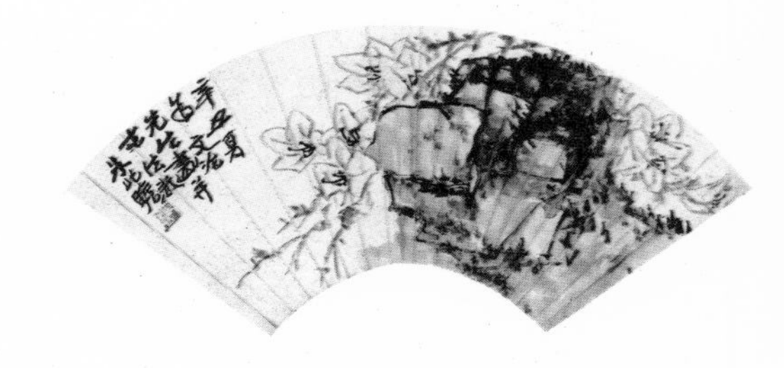

淺紅色的杜鵑花，淡墨的岩石，在看來不經意而實則苦心經營的筆觸和布局，正是老畫家功力深到的作品。朱屺瞻老辣蒼勁的用筆，不是一般畫家隨意可以做到的。

This plant among rocks represents the painter Zhu Qizhan's unique concept, composition and arrangement of nature's beauty. His painstaking, firm and skilful wielding of the painting brush have seldom been paralleled.

70. 紅 梅　**Red Plum Blossoms**

陳衡恪(1876－1923)是天才横溢而短命的畫家，他是齊白石、徐悲鴻的朋友，用筆受到吴昌碩的影響。這幅紅梅扇面，筆墨不多，但很有精神；梅枝是用書法的筆觸表現的，剛勁有力。全幅也都是詩、書、畫的結合，是典型的文人畫。

Chen Henglao (1876-1923), a most talented painter was, alas, short-lived. A friend of the masters Qi Baishi and Xu Beihong, he was also inspired by Wu Changshi in the wielding of the painting brush. These red-tinged plum blossoms do not carry much ink but are sprightly none the less. The twigs are no more than a few touches of the brush which bring out their essence — the ability to withstand winter's cold. When a man of letters paints, he combines his painting with calligraphy and poetry in one breath.

71. 芙蓉臘嘴鳥　**Cottonrose and Ivory-beaked Bird**

此圖的芙蓉花和46圖同，臘嘴鳥和56圖同，但表現的方法並不一樣。這幅畫的作者徐紹青(1919－)他的風格在中國畫中叫做工筆雙鈎的畫法，它盛行於十二、三世紀的宋代。這種風格要求工細而不呆板，適宜於表現静的氣氛。

The flower in this painting is the same as in picture 46, the bird in picture 56. The technique, however, is different. Xu Shaoqing (1919-) paints in a style called *Gong Bi* (realistic painting characterised by fine brushwork and attention to detail) co-ordinated with *Double Gou* (multiple lines giving the outline of an object), which was in vogue in the 12th and 13th centuries during the Song dynasty. Though detail is given full recognition, there is no rigidity or dullness. The technique spells tranquility.

72. 紅葉小鳥　**Red Leaves and Bird**

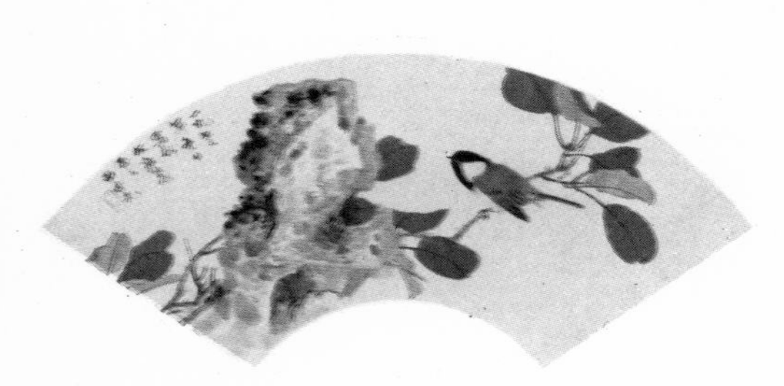

田世光（1916－）是一位工筆花鳥畫家，這幅花鳥畫表現出晚秋天氣中巢石、紅葉和小鳥的生態。作者對於花鳥有細緻的觀察，所以能够表現它的精神。田世光是住在北京郊外的一位畫家，中央美術學院的教師。

Tian Shiguang (1916-) is a realist painter who stresses detail in his flowers and birds. Here, in late autumn a little bird perches on the stem of red leaves beside its nest in the cranny of a rock. The painter is a keen observer of flowers and birds, and so is able to depict them faithfully. He lives in the suburbs of Beijing and teaches in the Central Fine Art Academy.

73. 芙蓉花　**Cottonroses**

這是同一以芙蓉爲題材而表現方法完全不同的一幅扇面。用比較寫意的筆調鈎出芙蓉及枝葉，上面的葉上站立一只形態如生的螳螂，頓錯有緻的中國畫筆神妙地賦予它以生命力。作者張辛稼(1909－)是蘇州的一位老畫家，現任蘇州國畫館館長。

The technique employed in picturing these cottonroses is a bold contouring of leaves in a darker shade as contrasted with the flowers in a lighter one. The mantis atop a leaf becomes as though alive, bringing the leaves and flowers along with it as if by magic. The painter, Zhang Xinjia (1909-), is Director of the Suzhou Academy of Chinese painting.

收 藏 家 小 傳

宋文治，江蘇太倉縣人，生於1919年，曾從事美術教育工作十餘年。1957年江蘇省國畫院建立時任副畫師。現任江蘇省國畫院畫師、副院長，並任中國美術家協會理事、中國美術家協會江蘇省分會副主席和浙江省杭州西冷印社副社長等職。

太倉是中國清初“婁東畫派”（即“四王”山水畫派）的發源地。三十年代至五十年代初，他從學“四王”入手自習傳統山水技法，並進而學習宋代李唐、元代王蒙、明代唐寅等大家的筆法。在業餘之暇又向海上名畫家吴湖帆、張石園、陸儼少請益，打下了中國傳統繪畫的基礎。六十年代至八十年代，他不斷深入生活，行程萬里，飽覽祖國名山大川，在山水畫的推陳出新上進行了探索。

1961年《山河新貌》畫展在北京展出，他的“山川巨變”、“嘉陵江上”等作品得到好評，這是他在創作上的一個重要轉折點。之後，由於他繼續研究傳統，不斷創新，虚心學習古今各家之長，又善於吸收外國繪畫的光、色處理技法，因而在數十年的刻苦實踐中逐步形成了自己的風格，創作出了許多筆墨秀麗凝重，意境清新雄峻的作品，尤以江南水鄉景色著稱。

他的作品曾參加國内外展出，並在中外各種刊物上發表，還被中國美術館和國内外一些博物館收藏。出版有《宋文治作品選集》、《宋文治山水畫輯》等。

Biographical Sketch of Mr. Song Wenzhi, a Connoisseur of Paintings

Mr. Song Wenzhi, a native of Taichang county in Jiangsu province, was born in 1919. He has been engaged in fine arts education for over ten years. In 1957, when the Jiangsu Provincial Academy of Chinese Painting was established, he was made Associate Painter. He is now Painter and Vice-Director of the Academy and concurrently a council member of the All-China Association of Fine Art Workers, Vice-Chairman of the Jiangsu provincial branch of the All-China Association of Fine Art Workers.

Taichang county is the place of origin of the Loudong School of Painting which flourished in the early Qing dynasty (the "Four Wangs " of landscape painting). From the 1930s to the 1950s Mr. Song first studied the technique of the "Four Wangs", then proceeded to imitate the styles of Li Tang of the Song dynasty, Wang Meng of Yuan, Tang Yin of Ming and other traditional painters. He also kept in touch with such famous painters of Shanghai as Wu Hufan, Zhang Shiyuan and Lu Yanshao, and profited by their instruction to build his knowledge of traditional Chinese painting arts and techniques. From the 1960s to 1980s he toured the country, experiencing realities of life, visiting mountains and waters, conceiving new techniques of landscape painting in new lights.

In 1961, *China's New Look* exhibition of paintings was held in Beijing. Here Mr. Song's paintings *Changed Aspect of Mountains and Waters* and *On the Jialing River* received favourable comment, inspiring him to further improve his art. He continued his study of traditional painting, learned new techniques, co-ordinated the merits of different painters ancient and modern, absorbed new insight from Western painting, and acquired advanced colouring techniques. In short, out of decades of theoretical study and assiduous practice Mr. Song evolved a style of his own in which he has created a number of artistic works which are clear and delicate, significant and imposing. His scenes of southern "water country" are particularly admired.

Mr. Song's artistic works have been displayed at art exhibitions in China and other countries, reproduced in Chinese and other magazines, and collected by the China Fine Arts Gallery and foreign museums. Among the publications of his paintings are *A Selection of Song Wenzhi's Paintings* and *Landscapes by Song Wenzhi*.

中國畫技法名詞簡釋

水墨畫　中國畫中純用水和墨畫出的作品。這種畫技法要求高，是鑒别一個畫家功力深淺的重要標準。以筆法爲主導，充分發揮水和墨的功能，取得"墨分五色"的藝術效果。這一畫體在中國畫史上占有重要的地位。

墨分五色　中國畫的技法術語，也就是中國古代畫論中所説的"如兼五彩"的意思。所謂"五色"，説法不一，有指焦、濃、重、淡、清五種墨色，也有指濃、淡、乾、濕、黑。

筆墨　中國畫技法和理論上的術語。技法上，筆指鈎、勒、皴、點等筆法，墨指烘、染、破、積等墨法。理論上，强調筆爲主導，但須與墨有機結合，才能完美地表現物像，表達意境。

工筆　中國畫中屬於工整細致一類的畫法，畫出的作品大都是色彩艷麗，線條遒勁，如31圖《春艷》。

寫意　與"工筆"對稱，屬於縱放一類的畫法，要求通過簡練的筆墨，寫出物像的形神。其中又有"大寫意"和"小寫意"之分。前者如1圖《荷花鴨子》，筆墨豪放；後者如58圖《雄鷄牽牛花》，近於寫意的筆調。

鈎勒　通常用於工筆花鳥畫的一種技法。用筆順勢爲鈎，逆勢爲勒；也有以單筆爲鈎，復筆爲勒。一般指用線條鈎描物像輪廓，也叫"雙鈎"，鈎勒後大都要填着色彩。

没骨　不用墨線鈎勒，直接以彩色描繪物象，如60圖《茶花雙鳥》。

皴法　用以表現山水樹石的筆觸，如40圖《陝北一景》的山石和27圖《墨松》的樹皮紋理的技法，是中國古代畫家在長期的藝術實踐中，加以概括而創造出來的表現技法。

點苔　指用毛筆作直、横、圓、尖或"破筆"（將筆毛松開，無一定形式），或"介"字、"个"字等形狀的點子，來表現山石、地坡、枝幹上和樹根旁的苔蘚雜草，以及峰巒上的遠樹等的技法。

烘托　用水墨或淡彩在物像的外廓渲染烘托（如49圖《水蜜桃》），使畫面明顯突出。這種手法畫雪景、流水、白色的鳥等都可使用，能加强藝術效果。

渲染　用水墨（如18圖《雪山圖》）或顔色（如17圖）《蘇州姑娘》）烘渲物象，分出陰陽向背的一種技法。

破墨　指用墨的技法，用濃墨破淡墨，或用淡墨破濃墨，使墨色濃淡相互滲透，達到滋潤鮮活的效果。

積墨　山水畫用墨由淡而深，逐漸漬染的一種技法。一般是先用淡墨畫到一定程度，然後再用焦墨、濃墨分出山巒田畦的遠近層次。

Brief Definitions of Technical Terms Relating to Chinese Painting

Shui Mo Hua (ink-and-wash painting).

A type of Chinese paintings which uses nothing but water and ink, a technique that tests an artist's proficiency. The disposition of the ink and water depends on how the painting brush is wielded, that is, the painting brush represents the master mind ordering water and ink about. The desired effect is "five tints of ink". This painting structure is typically Chinese and occupies a prominent place in Chinese painting art.

Mo Fen Wu Se (five tints of ink).

This term has two accepted meanings in Chinese painting. Some painters say the "five tints" refer to: charrred, thick, heavy, thin and clear, while others identify them as thick, thin, dry, moist and dark.

Bi Mo (brush and ink).

This style has theoretical as well as technical significance. The brushing consists of three movements: *gou* (downward), *lei* (reverse) and *cun* (curving). Inking technique consists of contrasting tints, ink-and-wash, colouring thick inking varying thin inking or vice-versa, and gradual laying on of ink from thin to thick. The two techniques are organically related and combine to make an object stand out significantly.

Gong Bi (realistic painting characterised by fine brushwork and attention to detail).

This type of painting belongs to the genre of fine brushwork. The pictures are brightly coloured and vigorously delineated. (See picture 31 of spring peonies.)

Xie Yi (freehand brushwork characterised by vivid expression and bold outline).

In contrast to fine brushwork, this technique of freehand brushwork is much more efficient in bringing out the significance or spirit of the object by vivid expression and bold outline. Outline varies from "more bold" to "less bold". (See picture 1 of a lotus flower and a duck, illustrating "more bold", and picture 58 of a cock and morning glories, illustrating "less bold".)

Gou and Lei (movements of the brush downwards, upwards and sidewards).

This means wielding the brush in different directions so as to delineate a picture accurately and delicately. The downward turn of the brush is called in Chinese the "smooth way"; the upward turn, the "opposite way". *Gou* also indicates a single line; *lei,* two lines. *Double gou* means lines drawn to give an outline of an object. *Gou* and *lei* are generally followed up by colouring.

Mo Gou (absence of outline).

Here, no outlining of an object is done, but its contour is drawn simply and directly by applying colours which form an image. (See picture 60 of a camellia tree with two birds perching on it.)

Cun Fa (roughness, cracks, grains).

This technique of showing shading and texture of rocks and mountains by light ink strokes in landscape painting has evolved out of centuries of experience by Chinese painters. It is today a creative and unique form of artistic expression.

Diantai (application of the brush in different shapes).

By this technique the painter wields his brush to draw vertical and horizontal lines, describe circles and pyramids. He loosens the hair of the brush to create the forms he wants, incorporates the characters 介 and 个 — all combining to delineate mounds, rocks, slopes, moss and grass growing on trees, and trees standing atop distant peaks.

Hongtuo (contrast).

When water-and-ink or light tints are applied to a picture being drawn, its contour is brought into relief by the technique of contrast, that is, by one tint setting off another. This is usually employed in drawing a snow scene, a running brook, a white bird, or fruit. (See picture 49 of honey peaches.)

Xuanran (applying colours).

Water, ink, colours are applied in a painting to set off a chosen aspect by contrast, by shading one part and throwing another into sharp relief. (See picture 18 of a mountain buried in snow and picture 17 of two young women of Suzhou.)

Po Mo (mixture of colour-shades).

This technique is adding thin inking to thick inking or the other way about in order to bring out the natural tints of an object in a lifelike effect.

Ji Mo (gradual inking).

Applied in a picture of mountains and waters, the inking thickens by degrees, beginning in thin ink. Finally semi-dry ink delineates low and steep hills, fields and furrows, distant and nearby overlapping mountains.

中國畫繪畫工具簡介

筆

畫中國畫用的筆，一般分柔、健和柔健兩者兼有的三種。柔的是羊、兔豪等筆，彈力差；健的是狼(黃鼠狼)、獾豪,彈力强；兩種不同獸毛合制成一支筆的，叫兼毫，更容易使用。三種筆各有長處,又各有短處，畫家都兼備幾種。

畫花卉，一般是點葉用羊毫、勾葉筋剔花蕊用狼毫，山水畫中撇小草、竹葉必需用狼毫，但也不必拘泥。

作畫用筆，因要意酣墨飽，所以寧用大筆作小畫，不要用小筆作大畫，但也要根據畫幅的大小來選用。作畫時，筆不要老是泡在水裏，筆毛泡軟會失去彈性，畫不出挺健的筆力。

筆有長短鋒，一般講是短鋒易着力。作畫時要全開，如覺筆鋒太長，可把筆根用線扎短。筆用好後要洗乾净，並把筆毛抹乾理直掛在筆架上，以保持筆毛不亂。

墨

作畫用墨，一定要用油烟墨,不要用松烟墨,但松烟和油烟同時磨用亦可。

墨錠磨用後，不要浸在水裏，也不要放在烈日下曬，曬易龜裂。墨質很脆，一摔即碎,應小心,如碎了，可用濕墨膠合,乾後即粘牢。宿墨不可用,容易污損畫面，但再加研磨後亦可用。

紙

中國畫用紙，一般都用宣紙，也用皮紙。

宣紙種類很多，有生宣及加工的玉版宣，可視自己的習慣選用。宣紙又分單層宣、夾宣（即雙層宣)、三層宣，畫中國畫一般都用單層宣。宣紙上加礬就成熟宣，熟宣不吸收水份。皮紙紙質牢，經得起拖，但墨色易沉,色灰暗。

學中國畫首先必須學會掌握宣紙的性能。應該多畫，不斷熟悉宣紙吸墨的情形。

中國古代作畫都用絹，後來才用紙。作畫用的絹，是特制的，有生絹和熟絹兩種。現在作畫大都用熟絹，因爲作畫，效果比生絹好。

硯

硯台不管是端硯(廣東端州出産),還是歙硯(安徽歙縣出産),但求細膩、滋潤、發墨。過於發墨，墨粗易傷筆；過於細膩、光滑，又不易發墨。

硯台不用時要蓋好，不使灰塵沾污。發現留有宿墨，應即用水洗滌，切不要用指甲及硬物刮磨。

墨錠磨後不要放在硯台上，因墨内有膠，石硯又易粘吸墨錠，用力一拔，易使硯台表面被剥落。

顏　料

國畫所用的顏料分植物和礦物顏料二類，與西洋畫所用的化學顏料不同。它的色彩種類簡單，有赭石、花青、胭脂、藤黄、石黄、石青、石緑、朱砂、白鉛粉等，這種獨特風格的色彩，也是構成中國畫獨特風格的物質因素之一。

水

學中國畫，首先要摸熟筆、墨、色、紙四者各個的特性和相互關系，而起調節作用的另一個重要因素就是水。中國畫又稱“水墨畫”,顧名思義,“水”第一，“墨”第二，由此可見水在中國畫技法上比墨還更重要。因此學中國畫，要先重視水的使用，但水份的掌握，無現成的配方，衹能在練習中不斷的摸索、積累經驗。

Concerning Chinese Painting Tools

The Brushes

The painting brushes are of three kinds: soft, firm and soft-firm. The soft painting brush is made of goat's or rabbit's hair, which has little elasticity. The firm painting brush is of weasel's hair, which is elastic. The soft-firm painting brush, called double-hair, is both elastic and easy to use. Each type has its merits and demerits, and the painter usually has a supply of the three kinds to choose from according to the requirements.

For a flower or a blade of grass, the painter outlines a leaf with a goat-hair brush, draws in its veins and the flower-buds with a weasel-hair brush. In a landscape painting the weasel-hair brush is more often used than not to fleck in a small grass-blade or bamboo leaf.

The painting brush must be "loaded" with the painter's conception of a picture as well as the ink to create it. The brush is large in proportion to the picture rather than the other way round, the choice depending upon the size of the picture. The brush should not remain in the ink longer than the required time or it will be too soft and lack the springiness necessary to reflect firmness in the picture.

The length of the hair of the brush varies. The shorter it is the more strength is able to flow from the painter's hand. Loosening of the hair is generally done throughout its length. If the painter feels it's a bit too loose, he can bind up its upper part to suit. When a work is finished, the brushes are cleaned of ink and any detached hairs, then hung up vertically on a brush rack.

Ink

Chinese painting requires a quick-setting ink (made from soot of burnt *you* tree) rather than ink from pine soot. The two can be ground together, however, and used in a proportionate mixture.

The ink-stick should not be left soaking in water, nor should it be exposed to the sun to crack. An ink-stick is fragile and breaks easily, and so must be handled with care. Broken pieces can be gummed together again with sticky watered ink. Freshly ground watered ink should always be used; any left overnight is likely to smear the surface of the paper.

Paper

Xuan paper, so named after the district *Xuan* where it is produced, is suitable for traditional Chinese painting and calligraphy. A tough paper made from bast fibre of the mulberry is also used.

There is a variety of *Xuan* paper — crude, processed, thin, two-ply, and three-ply *Xuan*. Thin *Xuan* generally suffices for Chinese painting. Processed *Xuan*, which is not water-absorbent, is crude *Xuan* glossed over with gum-film.

Tough paper (*pizhi*) has greater tensile strength and is more durable, but applied ink-colour gradually recedes and fades.

A Chinese painter should acquaint himself with the nature and use of *Xuan* paper. The more he practises on it, the better he learns its scope of usefulness and water-absorbency.

In ancient times, before there was paper, painting was done on silk, the specially made fabric for this purpose being either crude or processed. Nowadays the processed type is generally used, as the effect is more pleasing.

The Ink-Stone (ink-grinder)

Whether a *Duan* ink-stone (named after the *Duanxi* county in Guangdong Province) or a *She* ink-stone (name after the *She* county in Anhui Province) is used, the thick ink-and-water suspension must be fine, moist, soft and fairly easy to draw. If it draws too easily, it runs on the paper. If it is not fine enough, it damages the brush-hair, if too fine it does not draw easily.

When the ink-stone is not in use, it must be covered so that no dust can settle on it. Any thick ink mixture found remaining on the ink-stone should be cleaned off with water at once. Never scrape ink off with the fingers or use any hard or sharp instrument on the stone.

An ink-stick should never be left on the ink-stone, for the gum in the stick hardens and glues it to the stone. Removing it by force damages the surface of the ink-stone, and even causes it to scale off.

Colours

The pigments used in Chinese painting, different from Western, are derived from either plants or minerals. The colours used in Chinese painting are simpler — generally reddish brown (burnt ochre), dark blue (cyanine), crimson (cochineal), bright yellow (gamboge), pale yellow, sky blue (azurite), mineral green (malachite), vermilion (cinnabar), leaden (white lead), and a few others. These mineral and plant colours give Chinese painting a material basis that contributes to its uniqueness.

Water

Learning Chinese painting requires first of all becoming familiar with the brushes, ink and paper, and pigments, to know their characteristics and interrelationships. Another element is the water used in mixing colours in correct proportions, it being borne in mind that Chinese painting embraces water-and-ink "colours", with water first in importance and ink second. The learner begins by becoming aware of the effect of appropriate use of water in Chinese painting. There are, however, no definite guidelines; all depends mainly upon the painter's own efforts, experience, judgement, skill.

目　次

CONTENTS

護封：陳佩秋　劍蘭　團扇　絹本
1973年作　直徑32厘米

書名題字：謝稚柳

責任編輯、裝幀設計：孫　傑

現代中國畫集粹

編輯、出版：朝華出版社
北京車公莊西路21號
印　　刷：中華印刷廠
上海澳門路477號
裝　　釘：上海裝釘廠
上海虹橋路554號
總 發 行：中國國際書店
北京車公莊西路21號

1981年第一版　84CE-552

中華人民共和國印刷

FY 85
OVERSIZE
ND
1045
.H845
c.1
FY 85
DEMCO

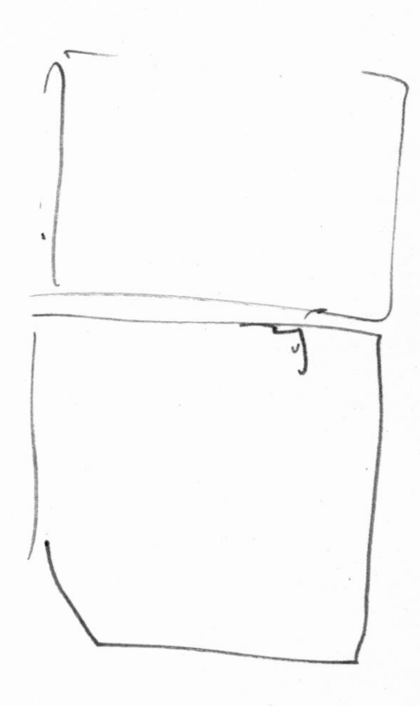